This is a book back to Robert Ward Johnson, my early instructor at the Art Student's League. This is a book back to Dr. Robert B. Greene, my anatomy instructor. This is a book back to Frank Taylor, my first editor, and Editor-in-Chief at McGraw-Hill Book Company. To Dickson Despommier, who published my book on Winslow Homer because he had faith in me. And most importantly, this is a book back to all my artist friends that have taught me so much. Thank you.

# Acknowledgements

I am indebted to my granddaughter, Lauren Demarest, for her help and guidance with the InDesign software used in the preparation of this book. Also, to William Logan for his support and enthusiasm throughout the entire project. To Carol Wolf for being on the other end of the phone whenever I needed immediate software guidance – which was often. To Doug Goodell, a reservoir of technical information and help. For Brian Soda an excellent graphic designer and willing helper and to Bobbie Golden, model extraordinaire, for her insight into the modeling world. I also want to thank Betty Pat Gatliff, superb forensic artist, and good friend, for her advice on facial types. I would also like to acknowledge Linda Barnes, expert ladies wear designer, for her advice on the shape and position of the female breast. And to my grandson and granddaughter-in-law, Tim and Amanda O'Donnell for their help in editing the book. And, I am indebted to my wife, Alice. Nothing would have been accomplished without her enthusiastic support.

# Index

148 illustrations

# The Anatomy of Figure Drawing:
## Secrets of a Master Medical Artist

by Robert J. Demarest

Chief Medical Illustrator, Columbia University,

College of Physicians & Surgeons (retired)

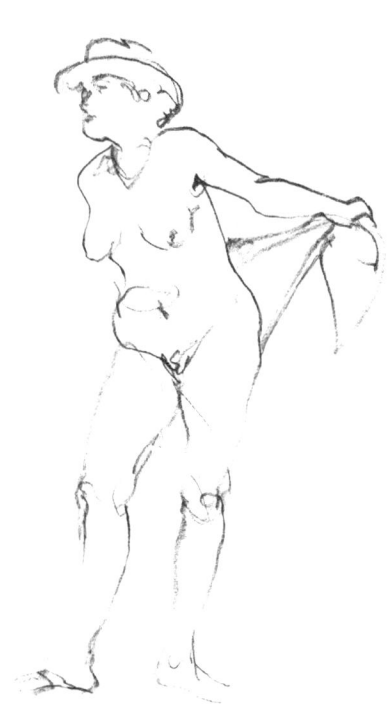

1

# Drawing Good Figures

I embarked on this book after a long career as a medical illustrator at Columbia's medical school, the College of Physicians & Surgeons, in New York City.

My office was less than a hundred feet from the dissecting lab at the medical school for much of my career. Working with the faculty at the medical school enabled me to immerse myself in human anatomy and I illustrated dozens of medical textbooks devoted to many of the major medical concerns of our age. I spent a great deal of time in the operating room, sketching the procedures for surgical texts or for publication in medical journals. Countless days dissecting cadavers led to a familarity with the human body privileged to few. It was a wonderful career and one that I cherish and reflect on often.

My time at Columbia spanned several decades– decades filled with great advances in the world of medicine. The advent of open heart surgery coincided with my entry into the field. Total Hip Replacement, the most successful surgical procedure in the history of orthopedics, came to Columbia Presbyterian Hospital in my early days there. My free time (mostly weekends and nights) was filled with freelance assignments for the likes of *Time, Life, Newsweek, The Saturday Evening Post,* and most of all, *The Reader's Digest.* I am "Joe's Liver, his Lungs, his Heart," and articles about many other organ systems became a successful, illustrated feature in the Digest for many years.

A typical medical illustration done during my time as chief medical illustrator at College of Physicians & Surgeons

However, while at Physicians & Surgeons I had no time to paint for painting's sake. No time for an excursion on a trout stream, and too little time for my family. So, one day, in my early 60's, I told the dean that it was time for me to retire. I wanted to test the waters of fine art, follow one of my idols, Winslow Homer, everywhere that he went, and fish and paint where Homer fished and painted. Little did I know, at the time, how extensively Homer traveled.

Along with my wife, Alice, we followed in Homer's footsteps for five years. Luck or serendipity led to many new discoveries in his life. Countless lecture requests at museums and art societies, and even fishing clubs, resulted in my book, *Traveling with Winslow Homer.*

All the while, even as I labored at the medical school, I attended life class, often at the Art Students League. After retirement, I was a regular at local art society life classes. I built a tremendous file of quick sketches, short and long poses, and many plein air watercolor paintings, most of which incorporated the human figure into the composition. I had used watercolor for my professional illustrations and segued into using watercolors almost exclusively for my fine art.

It was after an afternoon of cleaning and sorting my files and seeing many of my life class sketches that I realized my figure work had matured from constant effort. Of course, one thing about art is that the pursuit of mastery is never ending and, even as you improve, those victory goal posts are always just out of reach.

Did my knowledge of anatomy help me in depicting the human figure and using them in my paintings? For years I did not give that much thought. Instead, I spent my time refining my ability to draw the figure. I liked to put people into my paintings and I noticed that too few artists were really good at capturing the human body in paint. Too often their figures were either sketchily indicated or laboriously copied from a photograph. In just about every group show, I have seen paintings that were obviously based on photographs. The lack of discernment as to how to use a photograph as an aide in depiction, and not a crutch, seemed obvious.

*"Anatomy. that dreadful science! If I had to learn anatomy,*
*I would never have made myself a painter."* Ingre (1780-1867)

 I am convinced that knowledge of any kind can be an asset. However, I do not subscribe to the need to study anatomy extensively in order to draw good figures. That said, knowledge of a few key anatomical features, that make their presence known by careful observation, are welcome when drawing people. I have them in this book, and integrated the relevant anatomy into my existing sketches. My goal is to make you comfortable when drawing the figure. You can leave the fine points of anatomy to the medical world. Your world is, and should be, more concerned with observation and esthetics than learning the names of the bones and muscles.

Robert J. Demarest

### *You can't hide behind a line*

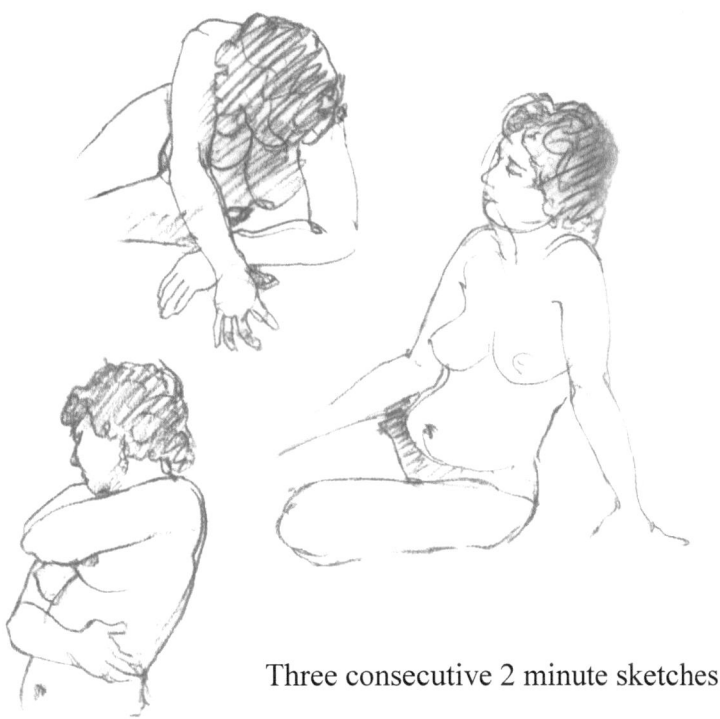

Three consecutive 2 minute sketches

All the drawings and paintings in this book are mine, unless otherwise noted.

# Materials

## *Sketching*

I use a standard spiral bound sketchpad for most of my life class work. The cost is reasonable and the paper is white. Colored or toned paper has the ability to fool the eye and make your work look a little more finished than it really is. I am most comfortable drawing with a firm charcoal pencil. I like the resistance I get from the slight drag of the charcoal on the paper. Any make charcoal pencil is fine. I sharpen them frequently during class, as they wear down quickly. Use an industrial razor blade or razor blade knife because a pencil sharpener can quickly grind up the pencil, often breaking the charcoal as it turns.

## *Contour Drawing*

I will, on occasion, use a fine graded marker pen for contour drawing. There is something definitive about an ink line that contributes to the discipline necessary for successful contour drawing.

## *Using watercolors*

For a longer pose, a cheap watercolor pad is fine. 90 lb. paper is heavy enough, 140 is better. Use the watercolor sparingly because drying in class takes a great deal of time. It is unfair to your classmates to bring a dryer to class, although I have used the electrical outlet in the men's room so that I can dry my work without disturbing the other artists.

## *Backpack and portfolio*

I recommend a backpack to carry your supplies. A palette, extra watercolors, spare pencils and pens, texture free paper towels, brush carrier, and water pans, all easily fit in, and you have free hands to carry a portfolio with your drawing pads and any loose papers. Balancing a fresh cup of coffee while carrying all this is still a challenge.

# Key Anatomical Landmarks in Anatomy

There are a few salient features that I will highlight in this section but knowing the names of a majority of muscles or bones adds little of value to the work of the figure artist. Every turn of the model's head, hand, or trunk changes the surface features. Knowing which muscle is contracting and which relaxing would be an all-consuming study for a kinesiologist, an expert in body movement, while of minimal help for an artist.

# Key Anatomical Landmarks in Anatomy

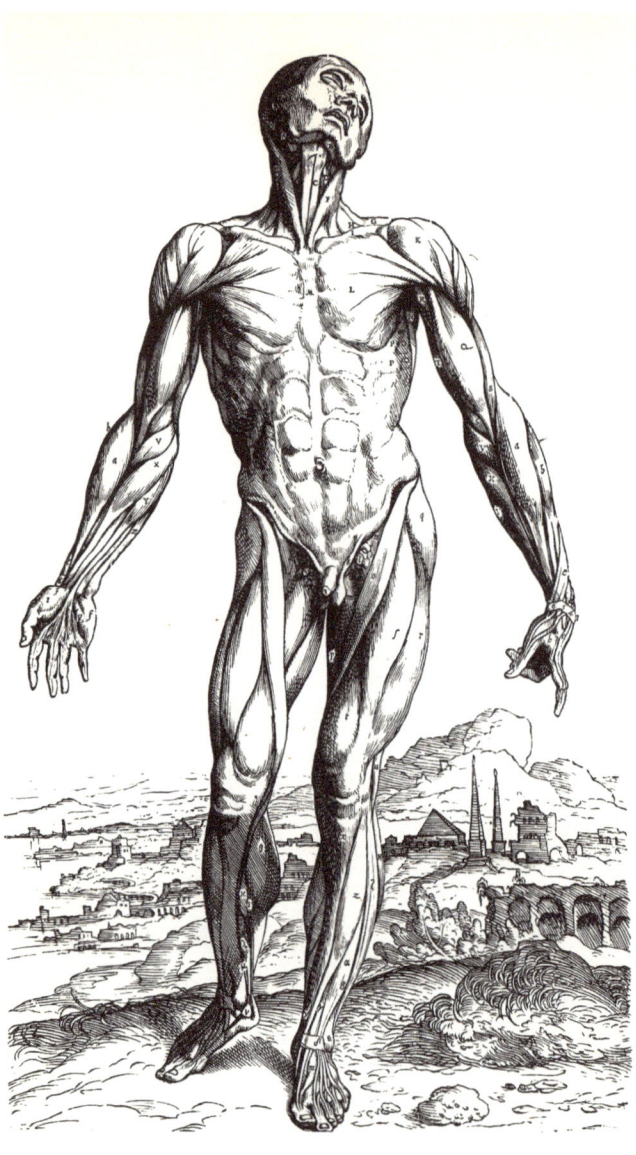

The first plate of muscles from Vesalius' De Humani Corporis Fabrica printed in Basel, 1543

I have collected a rather large number of books on anatomy for artists. Many have reproduced anatomical illustrations that go as far back as Vesalius (1514-1564) or Albinis (1653-1721). Almost all of them purport to help artists depict the human figure. While these illustrations may be of use and interest to a medical student or a physician, they are of little use to the artist. Most books on how to draw the figure seem to feel obligated to include some diagrams on human anatomy, and, in particular, the bones and muscles.

Many also show the body divided into blocks, or rectangles. The artist is supposed to use these blocks to "build' a figure. These systems bring to mind the ancient Egyptians and their use of squares and rectangles to fix the proportions of men and animals. They simply ignored the individual variations in people and relied, instead, on a formula that eventually came to be used for pictographic writing. It was a great idea when the ancient Egyptians wanted repetitive symbols with which to communicate. Our quest, however, is for dynamic, unique, individual figures and poses. Kimon Nicolaides, in his classic work, The Natural Way to Draw, says,

# *"Anatomy is the one subject that I do not advise the student to concentrate on in the beginning."*[1]

As a certified medical illustrator, I spent my entire professional career deeply immersed in the study of human anatomy. When I wasn't bent over my drawing board in my office, I was either in the dissection lab or in the operating room. In both places I was sketching the body, in the pursuit of knowledge and its eventual dissemination to the medical world. I got to know quite a lot about the muscles and bones, to say nothing about the organs and systems that contribute to this magnificent organism that we inhabit. You might think that I carry this information into life class. I can assure you, when I am drawing the figure, I think about it seldom.

Observation is the only path to successful figure work. Michelangelo's red chalk drawing, *Study for the Libyan Sibyl*, shows his awareness of the underlying back muscles but subordinates them to a *contrapposto* pose, twisting the entire figure. That drawing has been praised since it became known, not because Michelangelo knew his human anatomy, which he did - but rather because he knew how to pose a model and had trained himself to see.

## Anatomical Landmarks

The handful of anatomical landmarks I explore in this section will soon become familiar rest stops for your eye and pencil, on your way to a complete depiction of the human body. In life class, some poses will obscure these landmarks. Other poses will present some insight into the anatomy, as your pencil travels on its journey. For example, the clavicle will usually show its presence in many different poses. Rejoice in your recognition. The depression where the buttock muscles attach at the hip is a constant landmark and a friend to the figure artist. The way the muscles and bones move under the skin can be gloriously complex. Let them lay there unnamed while you look for a shadow or a dip on the body surface.

The human body works as a unit, every muscle and bone working in unison. They evolved to enable us to function as a successful species. For every muscle that contracts another extends or relaxes, always controlled, almost never in spasm. There is a muscular symphony playing in our bodies every waking hour. Our job, as artists, is to capture the music and not worry about the notes.

1. Kimon Nicolaides. The Natural Way to Draw (Boston:Houghton Mifflin Company, 1941). p. 145

The anatomical structures featured in this section are those that are obvious to the careful observer. By calling attention to them and featuring them here, I am giving you hooks on which to hang your knowledge without burdening you with superfluous material. The difficulty in transposing static anatomical charts to the living body is huge, and has turned numerous people away from striving for good figure work. Too many have given up on the figure after looking at the complexity of those ubiquitous anatomical charts.

*I have always tried to express the inner feeling by the mobility of the muscles... seize only upon the truth of the whole.*
*Auguste Rodin 1840-1917*

The complexity of the human body as it twists and turns for each action is marvelous to behold. The muscle contracts or extends as you flex your arm or leg. The bulge upon contraction is there for all to see (and draw). For many muscles, their action is more subtle. Fat can obscure the buttocks muscles. The femur is deep within the upper leg. You will never see any indication of many of the smaller muscles that attach to it. Instead, look for the nuance, knowing that every action affects, to some extent, the surface appearance of the body.

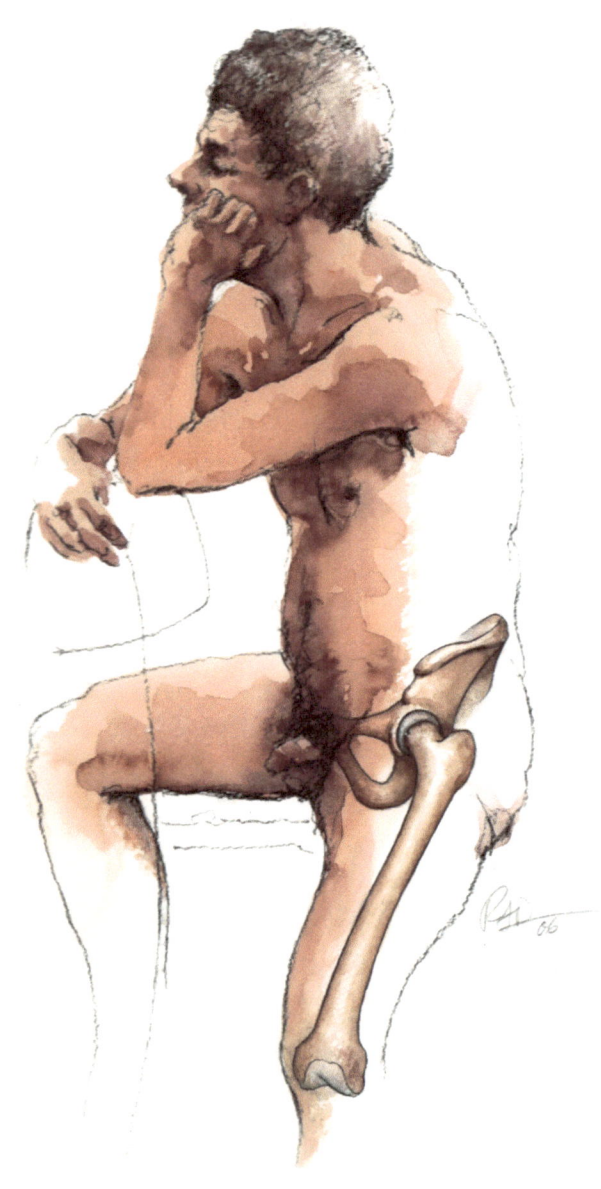

# Landmarks Worth Knowing

I have chosen a few anatomical landmarks that I believe are worth recognition. They can be comforting and should become familiar to the figure artist. They usually represent areas where our bony framework makes itself evident to the observer. I welcome them as friends, knowing that I will often be venturing out to less familiar territory with every change of pose and find comfort in seeing familiar structures whenever they become obvious. Every new pose will present you with a challenge, big or small. With experience, the challenges will become less daunting and often, not surprisingly, welcome. Remember, everyone would be a fine figure artist if it was an easy journey.

Many of the books on figure drawing carry extensive anatomical charts. Some even picture the small muscles buried deep within the body. Others show bones and views that only a surgeon ever sees. The anatomical features I have prepared were chosen because they make their presence known to careful observation. I have created new illustrations based upon life drawings I had produced previously. These new anatomical illustrations were integrated into the pose to highlight their significance to the movement shown. They are easy to remember and will help you navigate some poses because they contribute to the vitality of the pose and add veracity to your sketch.

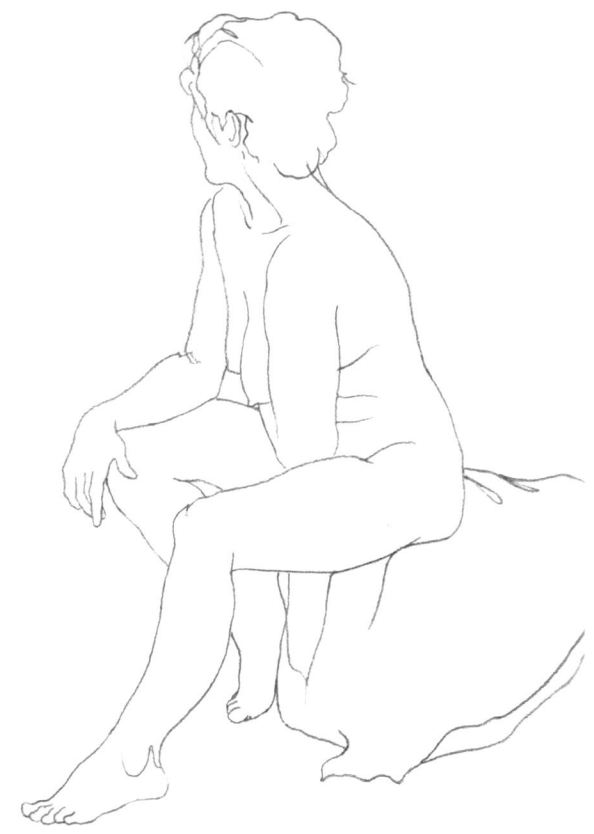

Even in a simple contour drawing, the clavicle and the sterno-cleido-mastoid muscle both make their presence known.

The following anatomical landmarks are arranged, roughly, from the head to the ankle. Again, I have used existing sketches from various life classes and fitted new anatomicals into these figures. No idealized figure was used because I want to show that the same anatomy may be common to all, but the proportions can vary with each individual.

# The Head

## How the shape of the face is determined

**W**hen you start drawing the head do not think of doing a portrait. You are not here to paint a portrait– rather you are sketching a figure of which the head is a part. Just draw. It's hard to say that, because everyone wants to paint a likeness right from the beginning. However, it is much more important to catch the energy and the uniqueness inherent in every subject's face.

When viewed from the side, some faces are more or less vertical, while most slope down and outward to various degrees, depending upon the prominence of the maxilla and mandible making up the lower part of the face. Artists should be aware of the underlying bony architecture because the shape of the human skull determines the shape of the face. I have used the generally accepted Frankfurt Horizontal Plane drawn from the upper edge of the ear canal opening through the lower margin of the orbit for horizontal orientation. This line, or plane, was established in 1884 by the World Congress of Anthropology in Frankfurt, Germany, hence its name. This line helps define a common horizontal orientation and the subsequent angle of the face itself. Three ancestral groups: European Derived, African Derived, and Asian Derived, are reflected in our population.

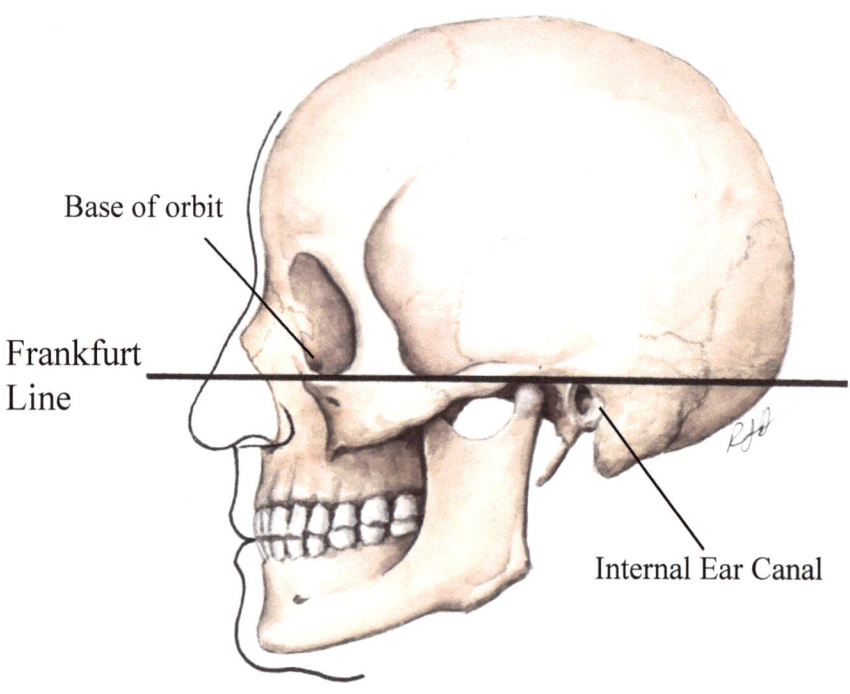

Base of orbit

Frankfurt Line

Internal Ear Canal

European derived

12

Artists should be aware of the differences in the bone structure between and within these groups. However, the differences that occur within these groups can be as great, or greater than the differences between them. However, when drawing different types of heads it helps to be aware of the anatomy behind these variations.

The shape of the head and face is infinitely variable and while anthropologists and forensic scientists have various tools and parameters to aid in determining ethnic origins, they are not rigid in today's populations. Intermarriage increasingly makes hard and fast rules about ethnic origin obsolete. However, for the artist, some familiarity with the underlying bony structure of the skull can be of help in understanding the basic shape of the surface features. With the exception of the mandible, itself a single bone, the bones of the skull are all tightly fitted together. The bridge of the nose is determined to a large extent by the nasal bone. It terminates in a peak and then gives the accompanying nasal cartilages the job of finally shaping the nose. For the proverbial "nose job," plastic surgeons often have to shave the bony protuberance, the nasal bone, in addition to shaping the cartilages. A "broken nose" can be a fracture of the nasal bone and or a break or dislocation of the nasal cartilages from the underlying, supporting bone. The jaw is usually more pronounced in people of African origin, while those of Asian origin usually present a flatter, more vertical face. Once again, you are cautioned to be aware that variations within these groups can be greater than the variations between them.

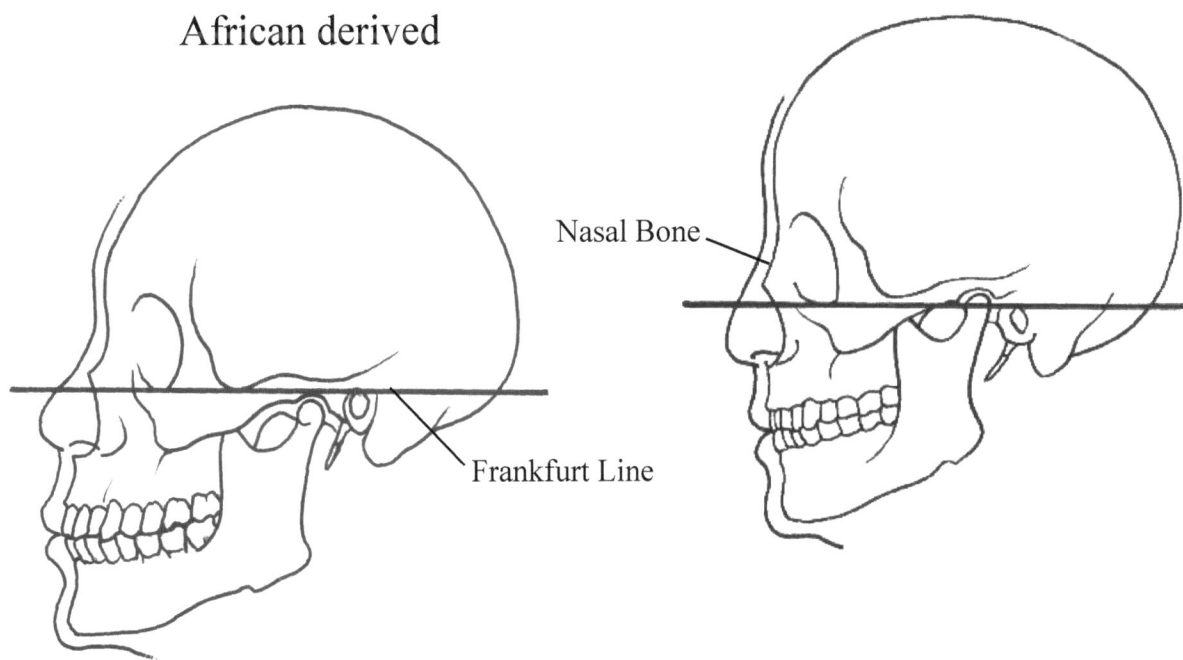

Asian derived

African derived

Nasal Bone

Frankfurt Line

# The Adam's Apple

The Thyroid Cartilage, commonly called the Adam's Apple, is most evident in the male. It is a cartilagenous structure that houses our voice box or larynx and is the entrance to our airway, commonly referred to as the windpipe. It has marched through history much under-appreciated. It has 3 main functions. First, the larynx contains the vocal cords that enable us to talk. Secondly, above the voice box opening is a flap that closes off the airway to permit swallowing, and effort closure, which enables stabilization of the chest, airway, and the shoulder girdle for sports and other physical pursuits. For example, in activities such as hitting a tennis ball, swinging an axe, or golfing, we close off our larynx at the critical time to enhance our action and accuracy.

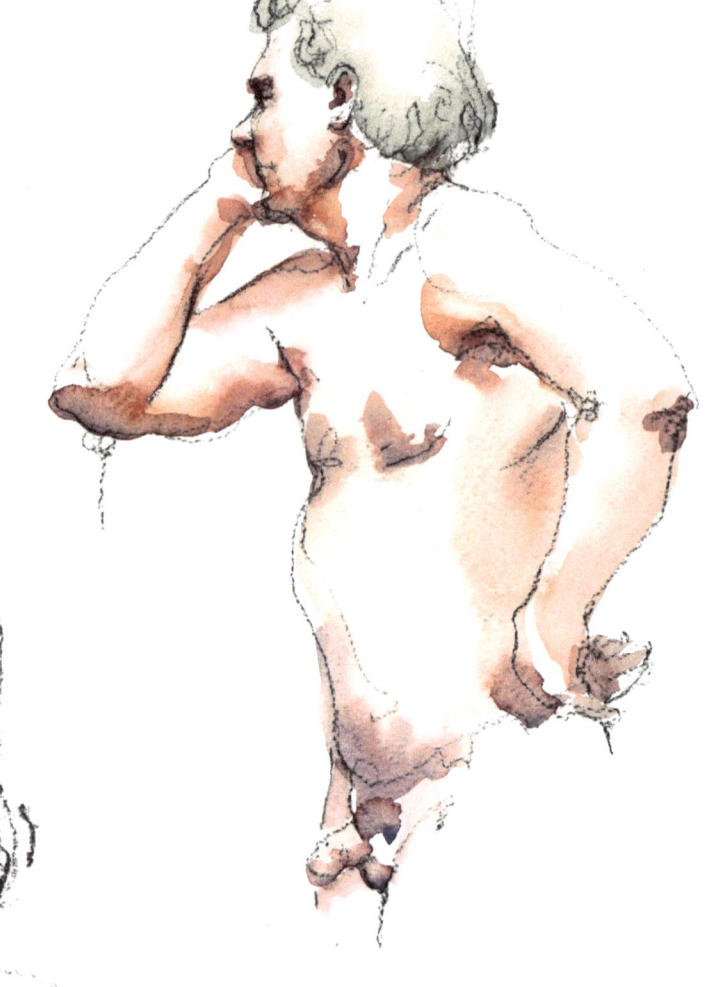

The Adam's Apple, or larynx, is more prominent in the male and as such is a secondary sex characteristic for that gender. Both sexes have a larynx but in women it is smaller, flatter, and much less obvious.

14

We are no longer using our physicality mainly to survive; many activities that are now sports were once feats essential to our survival.

Earlier survival activities such as swinging an axe, throwing a spear, or lifting heavy weights are now seen anew, with our hitting a ball, tossing a lance, or throwing the hammer in sporting events. The timely closing of our larynx contributed to our survival at critical times in the past and now helps us compete at sporting events.

Every time you swallow, the Adam's Apple rises, enabling that structure to meet an overhanging flap and close the airway. This happens all day, everyday, and most people are not aware of it. Just place your finger tip on the little thyroid notch in the middle of the neck, swallow, and your finger will ride up with it under your chin, protecting the airway. Of course, the mechanism is not fault free. We have all "swallowed something down the wrong passage" and paid a price for that. It can be a serious event and the evidence for that is the myriad Heimlich Manuever posters in restaurants around the world.

## The Difference Between the Male and the Female

The outer housing of the Adam's Apple consists of two plates of cartilage that fuse in the front, with a prominent upper notch. The two plates fuse at a more acute angle in the male; more or less at 90°, compared with about 120° in the female. Because the female larynx presents a flatter profile, it is less protuberant. It is also usually larger in men, which may account for the deeper male voice. It surely got its common name because of its prominence in the male. I am also sure that evolution played a large role in the gender difference in the larynx. Eve's Apple played an entirely different role in the Garden of Eden.

Today, transgender females often opt for a surgical procedure called a tracheal shave to reduce the thyroid cartilage so that their neck appears more female in appearance. It is a bit of a misnomer, as the surgeon is shaving the thyroid cartilage not the trachea. A prominent Adam's Apple is one of the more telling secondary sex characteristics. As such, it is a problem for a transgender person wanting to blend into the female world.

Portrait painters, especially, should be aware of its structure. It often shows itself in the opening between the descending sterno-cleido-mastoid muscles that converge from the mastoid bone to the sternal notch at the clavicle on each side of the head (see anatomical drawing). These two muscles work in opposition to turn the head. If the left side contracts, the head turns to the left. The muscle on the right side causes the opposite reaction. Look for the Adam's Apple in your male portrait work. It doesn't need much acknowledgment – just a soft line, small bulge, or a highlighted color will often do the trick.

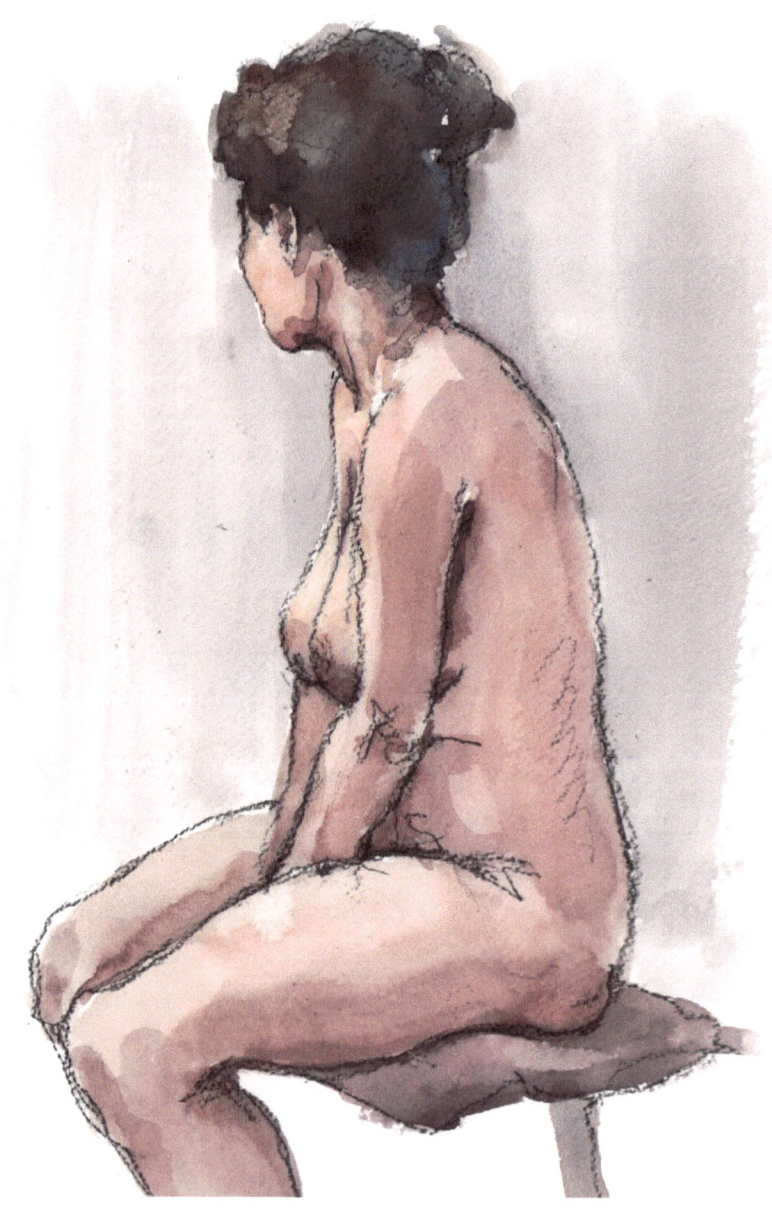

Most female models will not display an Adam's Apple and are probably very happy not showing that proturberant thyroid cartilage so common to men.

# The Sternocleidomastoid Muscle

The name of this muscle is a mouthful. It takes its name from its origin at the Sternum and the medial third of the Clavicle and its attachment to the Mastoid Process behind the ear, at the base of the skull. It is a paired muscle and the largest and most superficial of the neck muscles. Its function is to help turn the head from side to side when one side contracts, and to flex the head when both sides contract together. It also helps tilt the head. On some people it is very prominent and fun to watch as it makes its presence known with every turn of the subject's head. As such, it is a landmark to look for and an aid in depicting the turned head, giving character to the neck. In the male, the thyroid cartilage (Adam's Apple) protrudes from between this paired muscle.

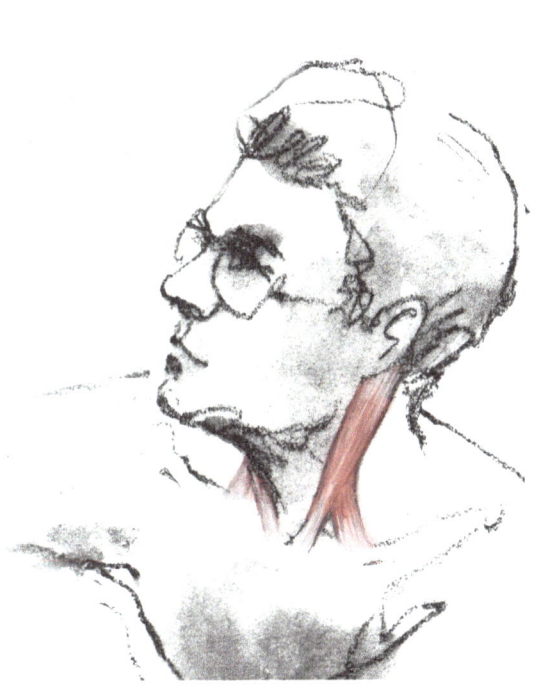

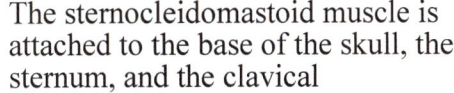

The sternocleidomastoid muscle is attached to the base of the skull, the sternum, and the clavical

Sometimes the Sternocleido Mastoid Muscle (SCM) muscle will stand out prominently. Other times, particularly in a woman with a slender neck, it will be hard to find. That's O.K. The owner of a swan-like neck is probably very happy that no muscle is evident there. It is only when the underlying anatomy is evident, only when it plays a role in capturing the essence of the figure, is it worth noting. In the accompanying quick sketch, a model displays the muscle as she turns her head.

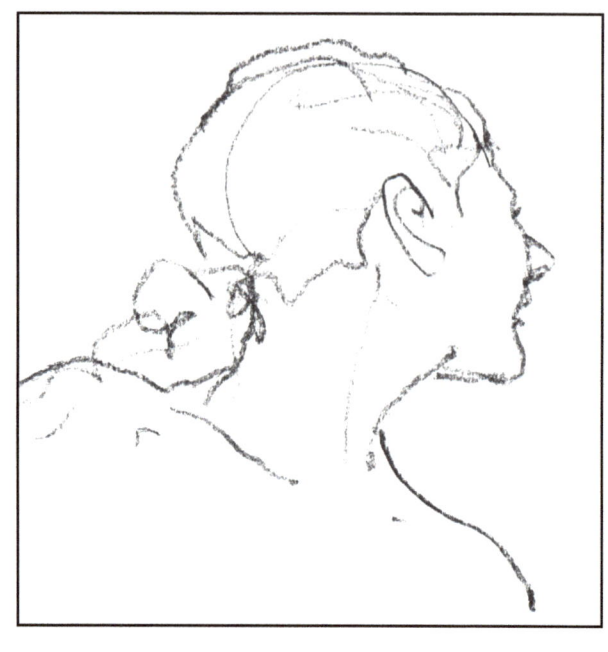

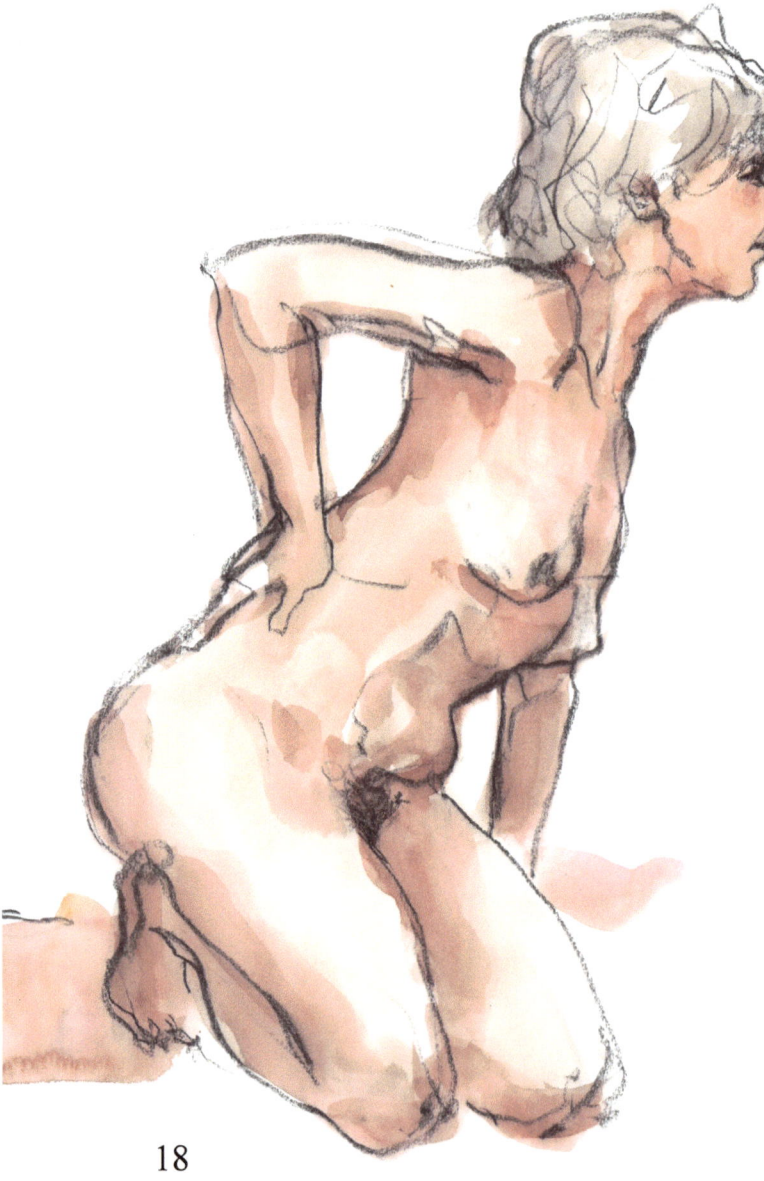

At times you might recognize the SCM muscle and record it simply with a line, sometimes with nothing more than a nod of your head, as you would a passing acquaintance. It is all about familiarity, comfort, and your judgment as to how prominently you feature it as you draw the figure. Just don't let it dominate the drawing.

18

# The Shoulder Girdle
## The Clavicle and the Scapula

The clavicle, along with the scapula, make up the shoulder girdle. The shoulder girdle is attached to the main skeleton, bone to bone, only in the front, at the top of the sternum, via the sternoclavicular ligament. This ligament allows the distal end of the clavicle to move up and down, while in the back, the scapula is held in place only by muscles. These muscles allow for a great deal of movement. The two bones are joined together by a ligament and form a protective shelf over the shoulder joint. One need only recognize the range of motion involved in the swinging of a bat, throwing a baseball, or simply bending down to tie tie one's shoes, to see the advantages in this flexible arrangement.

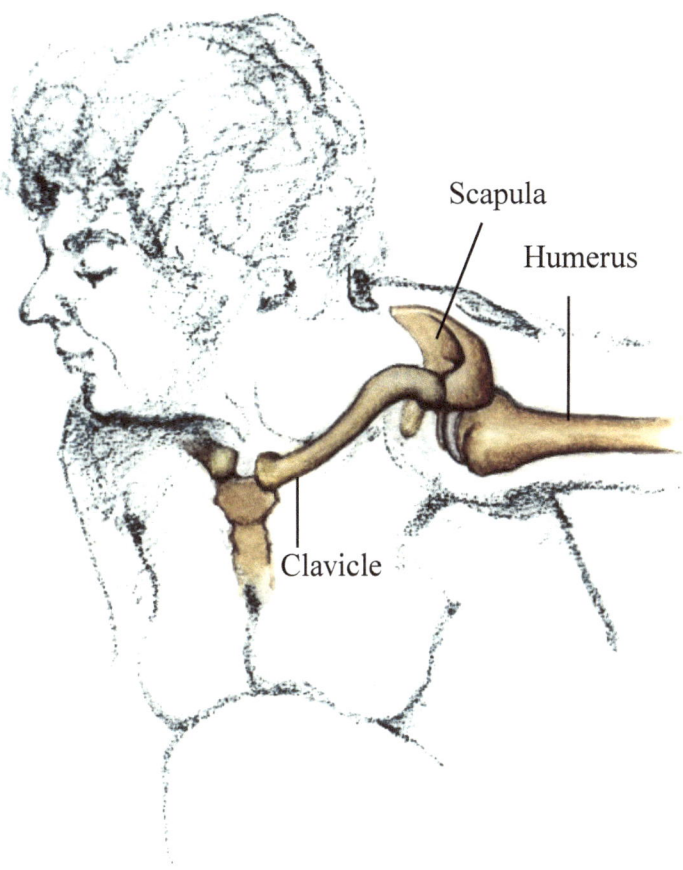

The scapula cooperates by helping position the glenoid–humeral joint (shoulder joint) in the most advantageous position for the task at hand. Bending down or reaching up and out is facilitated by the ability of the scapula to slide up on the ribcage, extending reach with the cooperation of the clavicle. The shoulder joint is very shallow, and this saucer-like shallowness aids in the arm's flexibility. In contrast, the hip joint, which is deep, is often described as a ball and socket joint. With its deep pelvic socket and an added attaching ligament, the leg can swing easily but cannot compare to the range of the arm's movement. Each extremity is beautifully adapted to its main functions.

# The Clavicle

The clavicle is one of the more important landmarks in life drawing. It's smooth curve around the upper rib cage and its sudden change of direction, so it can attach to the flat bony acromion process of the scapula, is usually apparent on the surface. Any time an anatomical landmark, such as this, presents itself, welcome it. The clavicle seldom appears as a straight line and while there is great variation within the norm, look for its characteristic curves. In order to keep the shoulder joint patent, a strong ligamentous capsule keeps the humeral head of the upper arm bone strongly attached to the scapula. Overuse or extreme strain can cause this capsule, commonly known as the rotator cuff, to tear or wear through, requiring medical attention. Most of the shoulder muscles attach to this capsule. For the artist, it is important to know that the joint is movable, allowing for a large range of motion. Every action of the arm will present a different look, once again emphasizing the importance of close observation. For example, you can only raise your arm to the side to a limited extent without turning your hand to allow the arm to clear the acromion process. This can affect how you draw a fully raised arm.

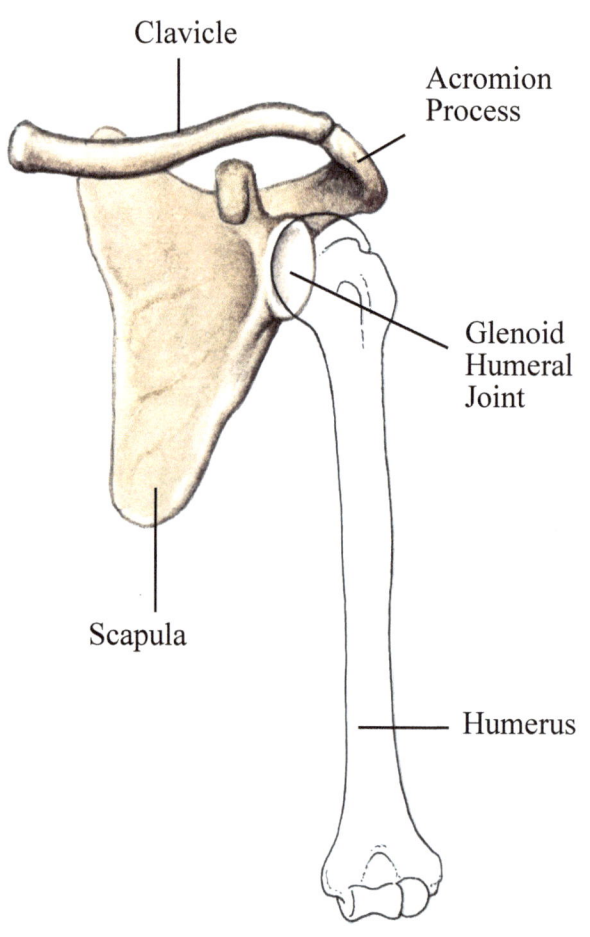

Clavicle

Acromion Process

Glenoid Humeral Joint

Scapula

Humerus

Standard anatomy plates show the scapula in the anatomical position (straight on front and back views). Unless you want to paint static and rigid postures you can't rely solely on anatomical plates. The scapula moves with every new position of the arm and the scapulae permit each arm to move independently. This means that the bulges and shadows seen on the back vary with every arm movement.

# The Scapula

The scapula compliments the clavicle, completing the shoulder girdle. The scapula is attached to the ribcage only by muscles, and can move over much of the upper back. This facilitates arm movement, as it can position the shoulder joint to advantage the assigned chore. In the inset illustration you can see how the scapula is able to swing outward and upward as it positions the shoulder joint to move forward, allowing the model to rest her arms atop the small table. Note the shadow on the figure painting, indicating the position of the underlying scapula, high on the back.

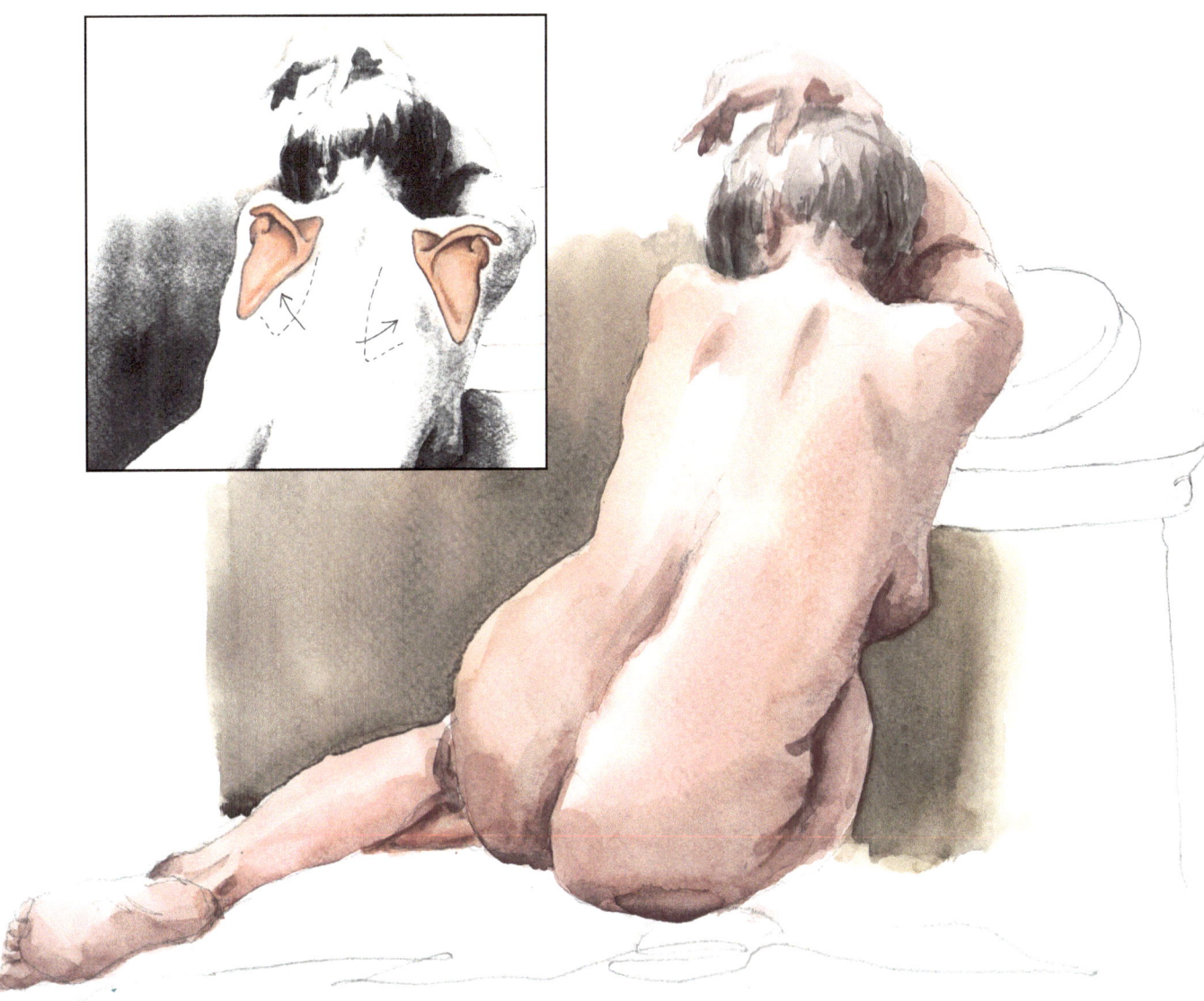

Every action of the arms will present a different look, once again emphasizing the importance of close observation.

For the artist, it is important to know that the joint allows a large range of motion, while altering the look of the shoulder area. The direction of the clavicle (collar bone) moves with the scapula as it slides over the upper ribcage. It is important to be aware that the muscles and bones can present differently with every activity and from every point of view.

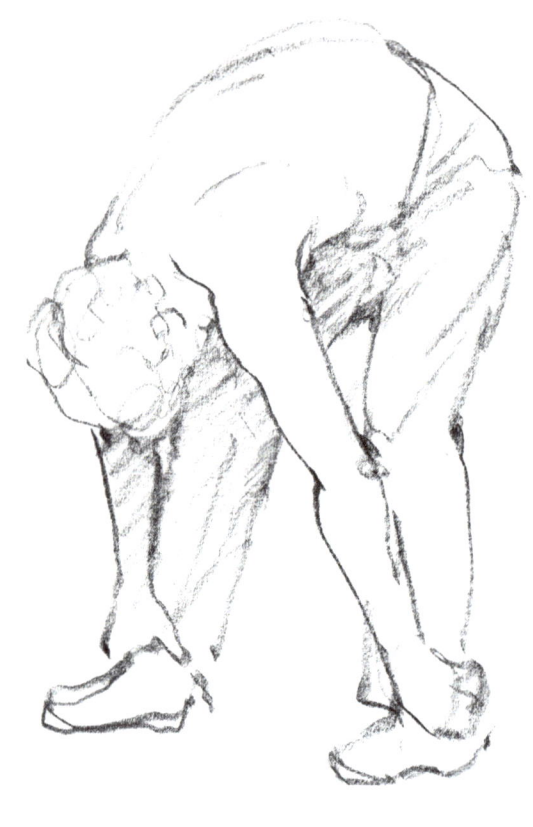

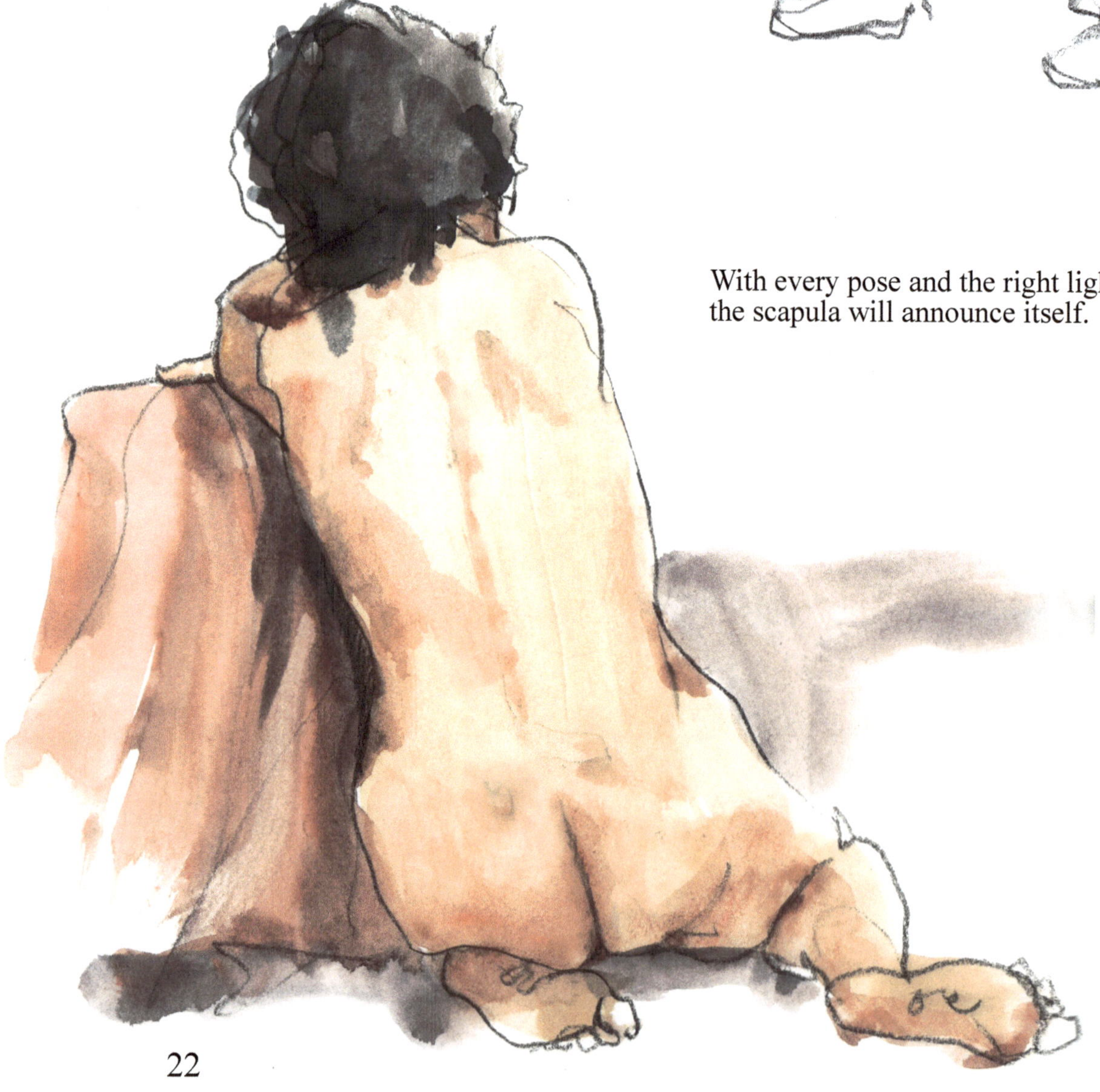

With every pose and the right lighting, the scapula will announce itself.

# The Humerus, Ulna and Radius

We're not going to dwell on the skeletal anatomy of the arm because it is pretty straightforward and most people do not have trouble drawing a credible arm. However, you should know that it is composed of an upper arm bone, the humerus, which has a funny name, derived from the Latin for shoulder.

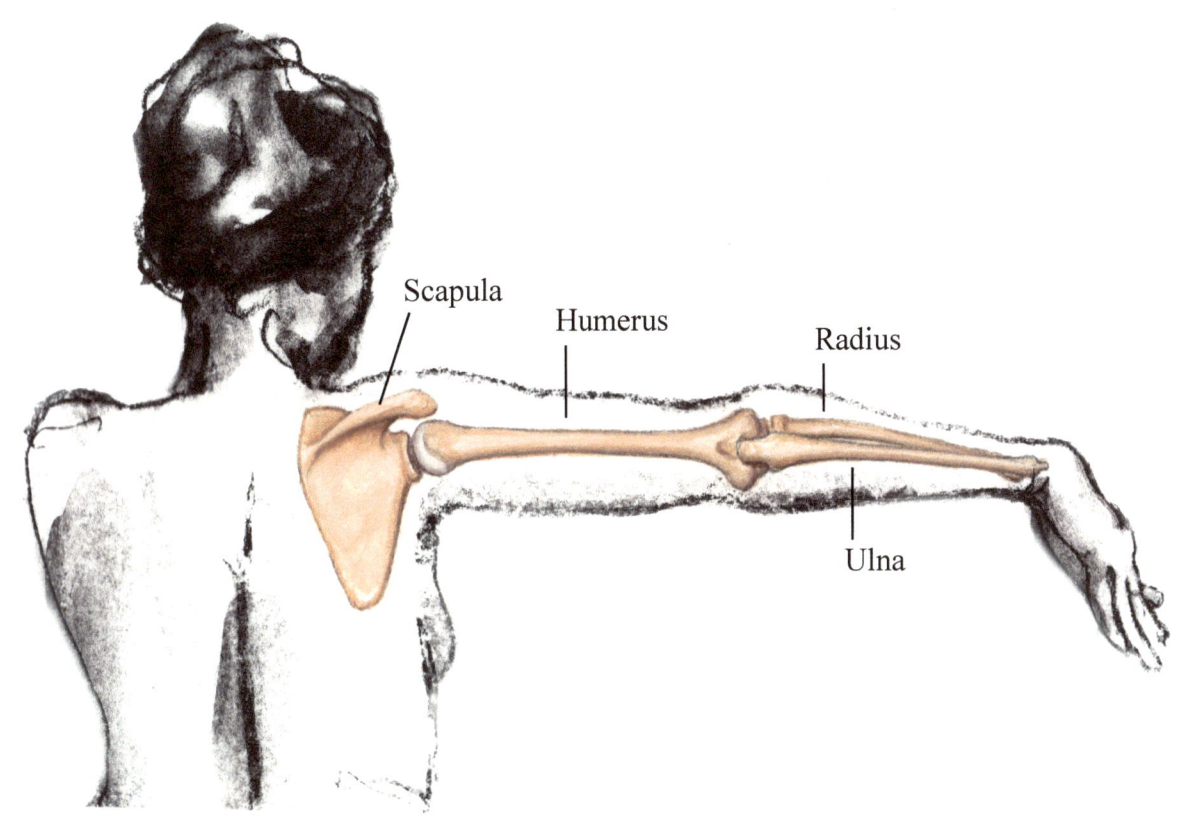

The scapula, humerus, ulna and radius, in that order.

There are two lower arm bones, one of which, the ulna, finds its name in crossword puzzles, because it has only four letters-two of which are vowels, and the radius, which does as its name implies, radiates around its partner, the ulna. This enables you to turn your hand, facing it up or down with ease. Grasping a pencil or brush, turning a knob, or doing any one of the thousands of hand maneuvers is easily accomplished because of this smooth anatomical arrangement. The lower arm muscles attach just at or below the elbow. These muscles do most of their work in the hand by way of their long tendons. It's a beautiful arrangement, freeing the hand for fine movements by having the needed muscle masses in the arm itself.

# The Female Breast

The female breast is a very variable structure. Just ask a foundation garment designer about the difficulty of designing for the various body types and ensuring a comfortable fit for every woman.[2] Most major foundation garment companies employ designers who work with lingerie models – models with many different body types, breast shapes, and sizes, in the pursuit of a comfortable, perfect fit.

Anatomically, the breast tissue itself is lightly attached to the underlying chest muscle by small fibrous bands called **Suspensory Ligaments**. The breast extends in greater or lesser degree up into the arm pit, in what is called an axillary tail. Additionally, a thin sheet of breast tissue often reaches as high as the clavicle on the front of the chest and may extend almost to the midline. The nipple is angled approimately 15° to 20° toward the side. This may be nature's way of helping mothers nurse a baby in comfort.

Over many years fashion dictates have altered people's perception of the ideal position of the breast and distorted its appearance. Push-up bras and under wires have given way to less restrictive under garments and, in some cases, no garments at all. Breast implants, now more popular than ever, have added a new element to the female form.

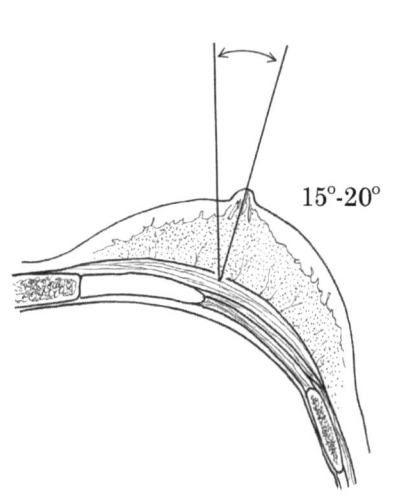

15°-20°

Cross section through the chest at the level of the nipple showing the nipple angle relative to the chest.

In order to avoid constantly rubbing the nipple, today's active women wear a brassiere that angles the nipple more forward. Many brassieres are purposely designed this way. Women in sports, in particular, appreciate this structural change in a sports bra.

The breast is dependent. loosely attached to the chest muscle, and moves with the changes in position of the body and the arms. Its appearance is affected by its mixture and distribution of glandular tissue and fat. Michelangelo's "Night" in the Medici Chapel, or his muscular Sybils in the Sistine Chapel, look like male bodies with breasts pasted on a male chest.

2. Phone call to garment designer. 3/17/2016

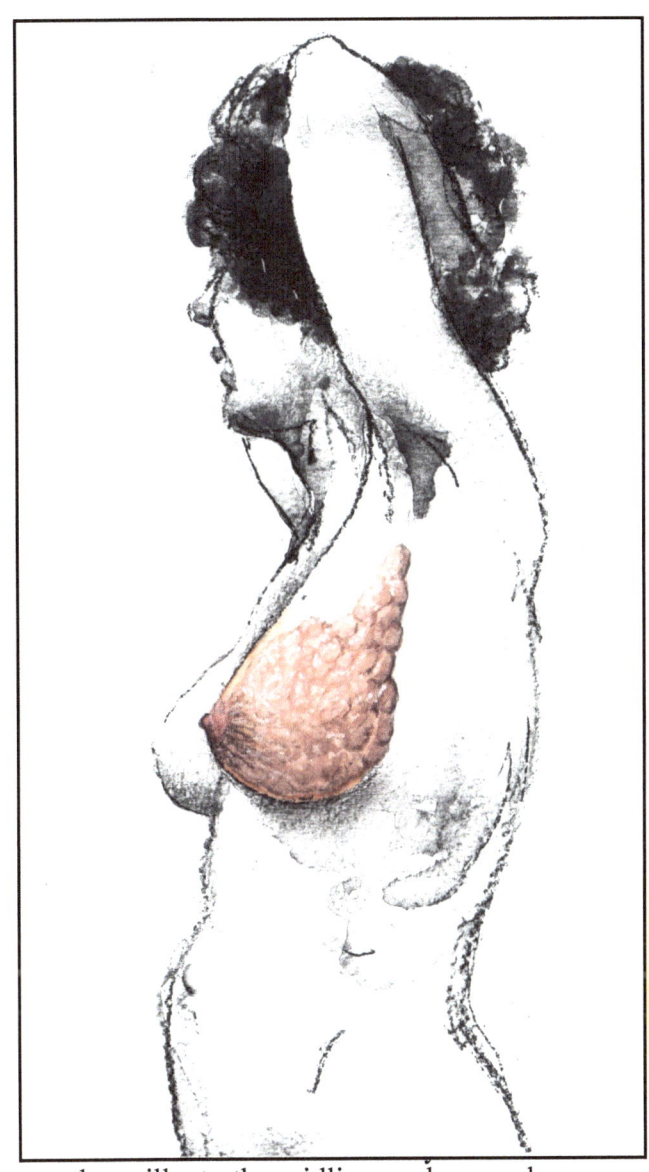

the axilla, to the midline, and upwards as far as the clavicle.

They are unnatural looking, to say the least. This has led to conjecture and explanations ranging from Michelangelo's sexuality to mores in the early Renaissance. Today, his depictions look unrealistic.

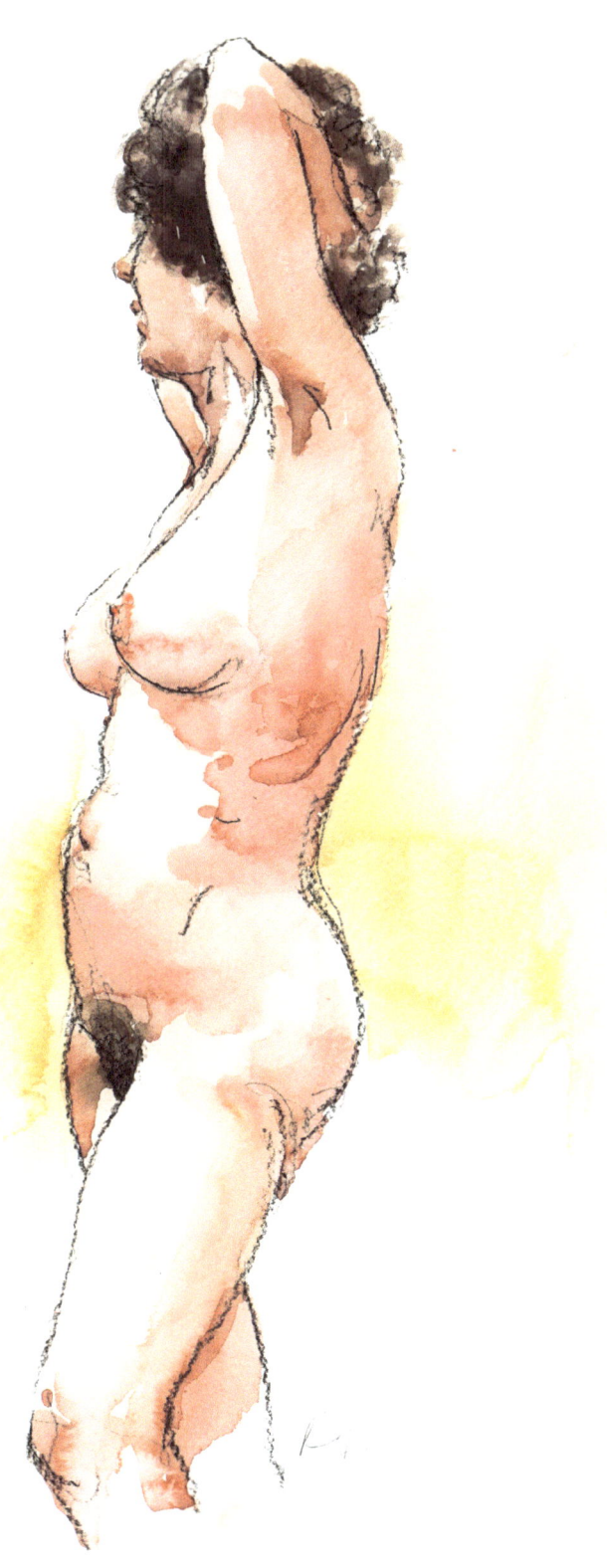

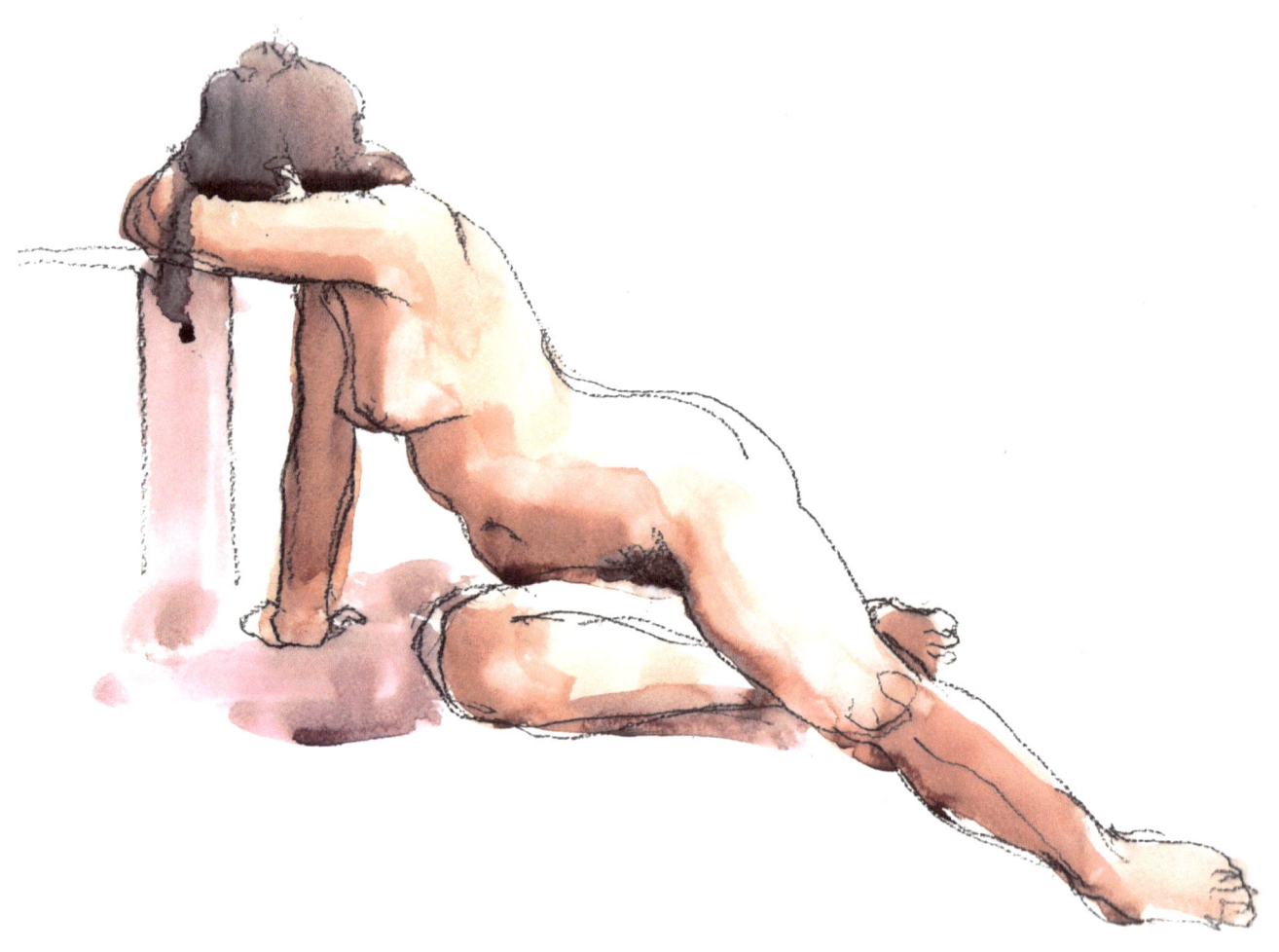

## Plastic Surgery

It does seem that more than a few plastic surgeons have succumbed to societal pressure and feature breast augmentation procedures in their practice. Some have been known to disregard basic female anatomy in their desire to please their patients. In contrast, a number of women are now having breast reduction surgery, enabling some to avoid having to wear a bra at all. Breast reconstruction after cancer surgery is, of course, an invaluable service to women.

On occasion, a life model with breast implants arrives at class and the change in the way the breast moves, or should move is immediately obvious to the students. For the artist, it is something to be aware of, noticed in silence, and, at times to be chagrinned by the loss of the natural movement of the breast.

# Rectus Abdominus muscle

**A** strong membranous sheath encloses the Rectus Abdominus muscle. Young, virile men like to show it off. When well developed, because of its segmented structure, it is referred to as a "six-pack." Women prefer their own softer appearance. Strenghtening it can help relieve back strain but a strong Psoas Muscle, unseen, inside the abdomen, may supply real benefit for the back, from the same exercises.

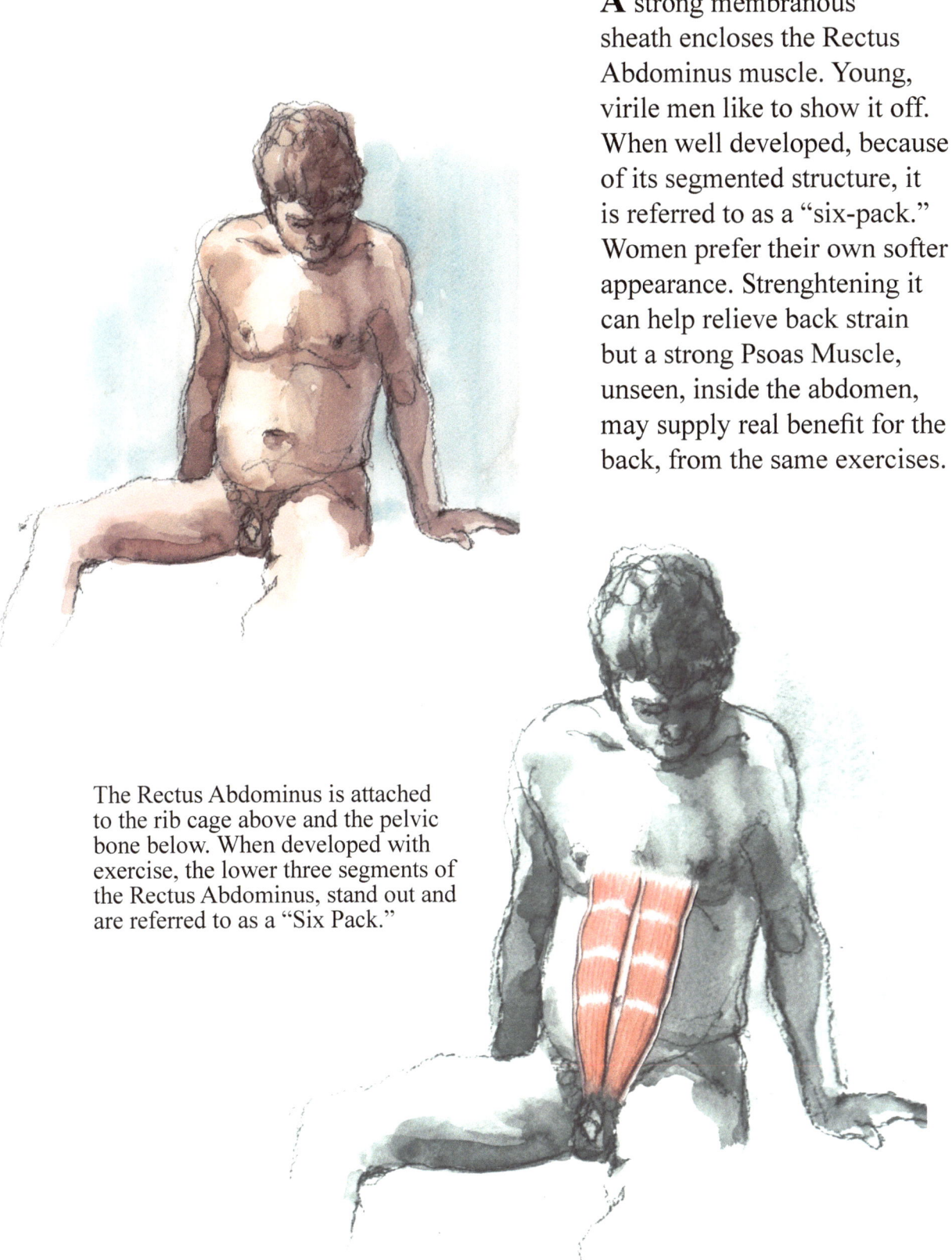

The Rectus Abdominus is attached to the rib cage above and the pelvic bone below. When developed with exercise, the lower three segments of the Rectus Abdominus, stand out and are referred to as a "Six Pack."

# The Vertebral Column – Cervical Spine

A great deal could be said about the vertebral column, not the least, that your back or neck will probably affect you at sometime in your career as an artist. Being bent over a drawing board, or an easel for a good part of your life will often take its toll. The vertebral column, or spine, is the core bony structure of the body but is mostly invisible to the artist. Its 24 segments, or vertebra, are separated by discs that permit the spine to flex and twist to a limited extent. The uppermost vertebra, the Atlas, has two shallow oval recesses that cradle the head permiting it to turn from side to side.

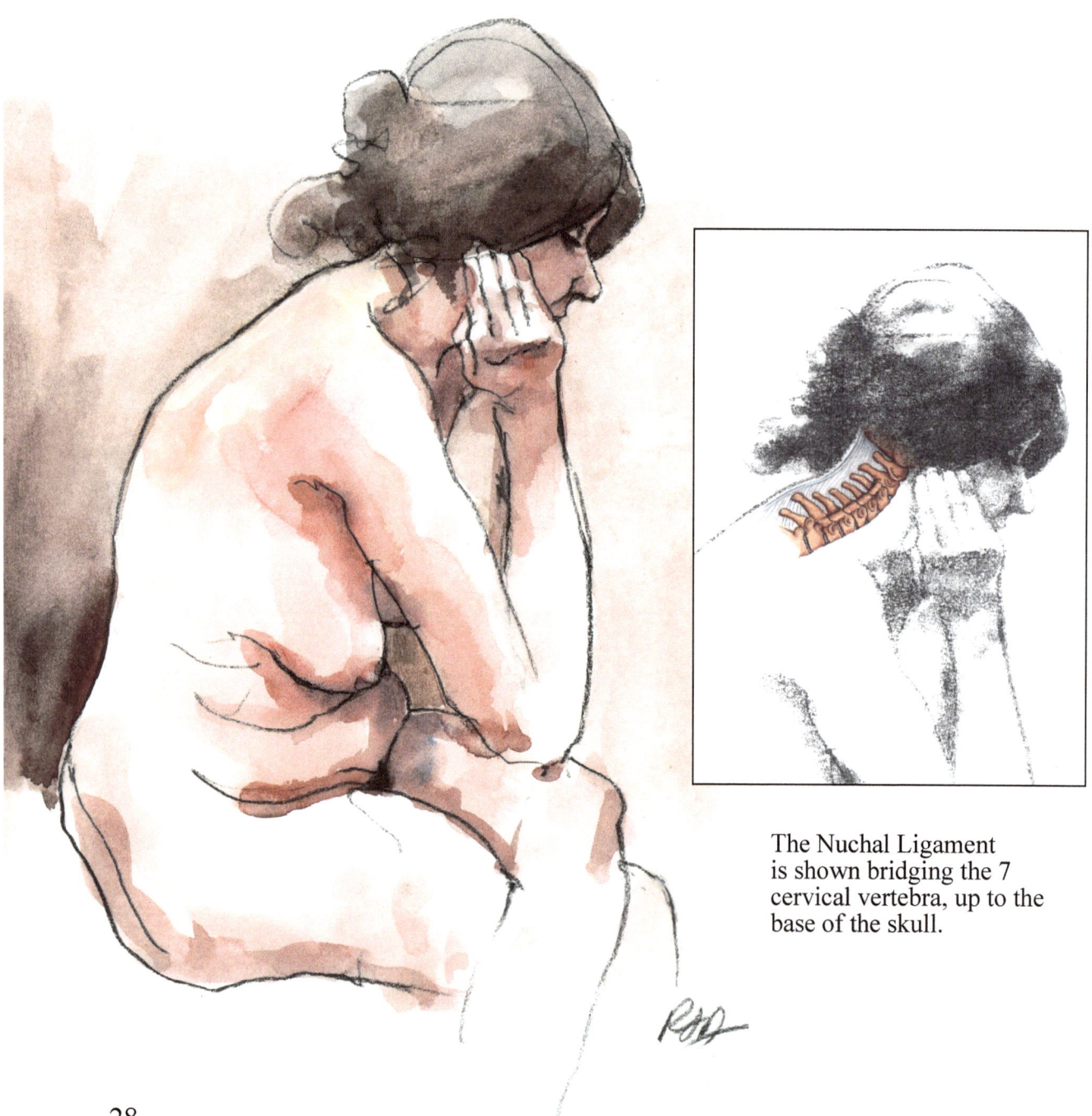

The Nuchal Ligament is shown bridging the 7 cervical vertebra, up to the base of the skull.

That first vertebra is named, in Greek mythology, for the Titan Atlas. According to the myth, the Titans were defeated in a war with the Olympians and as punishment, Atlas was given the task of holding the heavens on his shoulders. I am sure the vertebra we call Atlas carries our head with relatively more ease than the Titan carried the heavens. In addition, much of our burden is lightened by the Nuchal Ligament which runs from the base of the skull down to the 7th cervical vertebra. This ligament helps keep the head erect and, with the addition of various muscles, helps us respond to a sleepy nod by snapping us to attention. We've all seen someone nod off on a train, or at a concert, only to awake with a start after their head sags forward in a half-sleep.

## 7th Cervical Vertebra

The 7th and last of the cervical vertebra usually has the longest spinous process, and it acts as the final attachment place for the Nuchal Ligament. With the head bent down and the neck forward, it is easily identified by its prominence.

The bony spinal process on the 7th cervical vertebra is evident when a model bends his or her head down.

It is a landmark when you are drawing the figure from the side. Its prominence is a noteworthy marker that helps the artist navigate the complex human body. You can further appreciate its importance when you consider the Nuchal Ligament in a horse where it helps in holding up a very large head. On thin models you can easily see the tips of most of the spinous processes just under the skin, as they run down the middle of the back. However, none have the prominence or the role of cervical vertebra number seven.

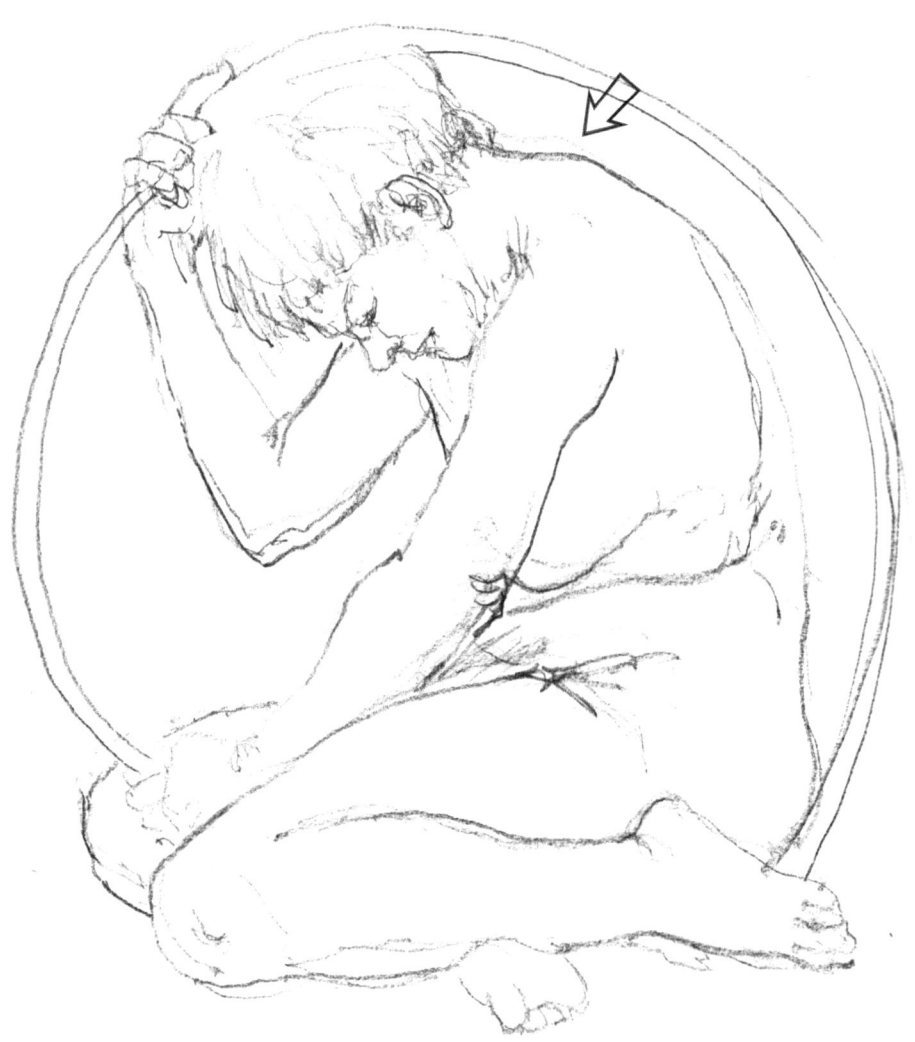

The model brought a plastic hoop to Life Class and used it effectively throughout the session. In this 15 minute pose, as she fitted her pose to the hoop by bending her head, the 7th cervical vertebra clearly showed it presence.

# The Complete Column

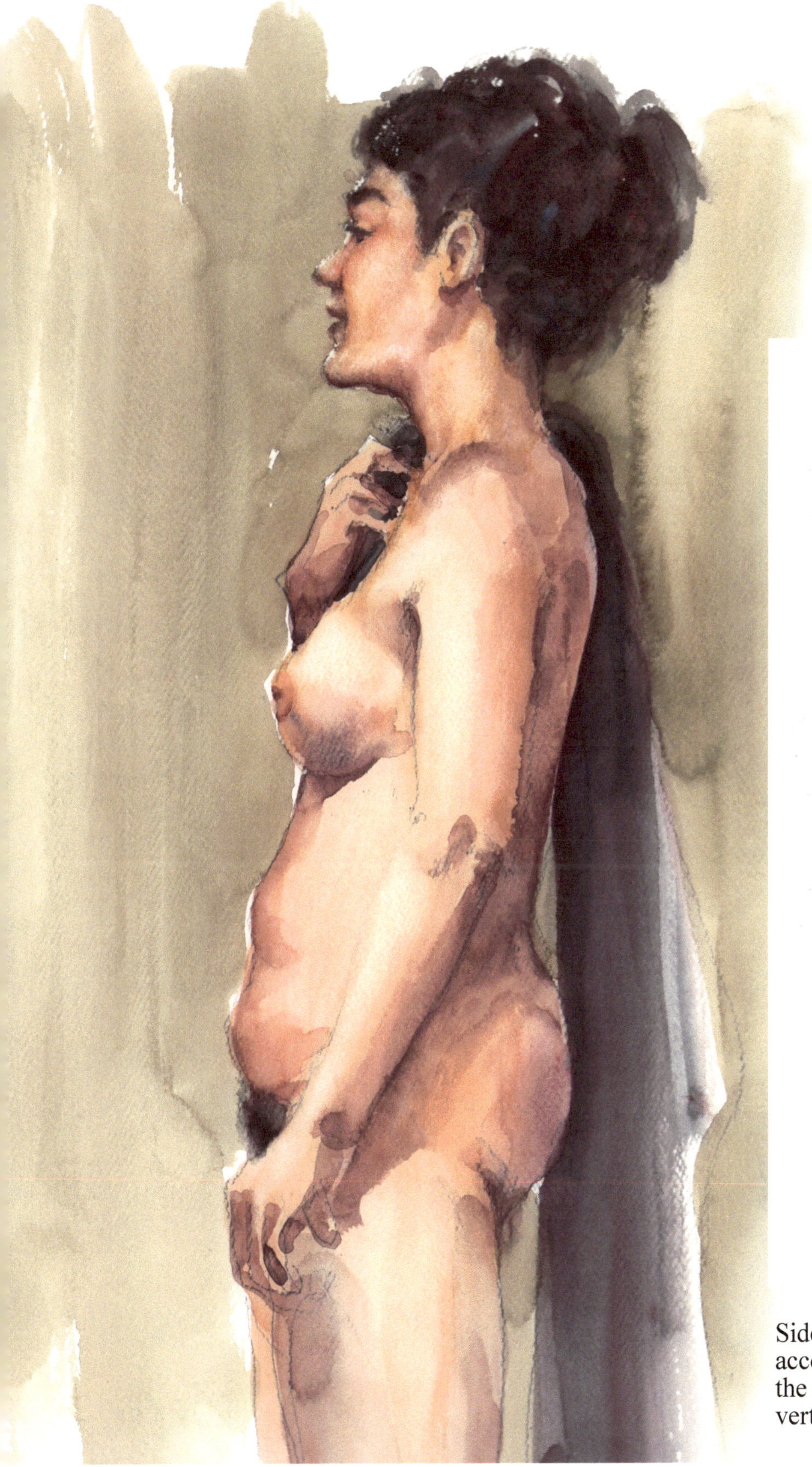

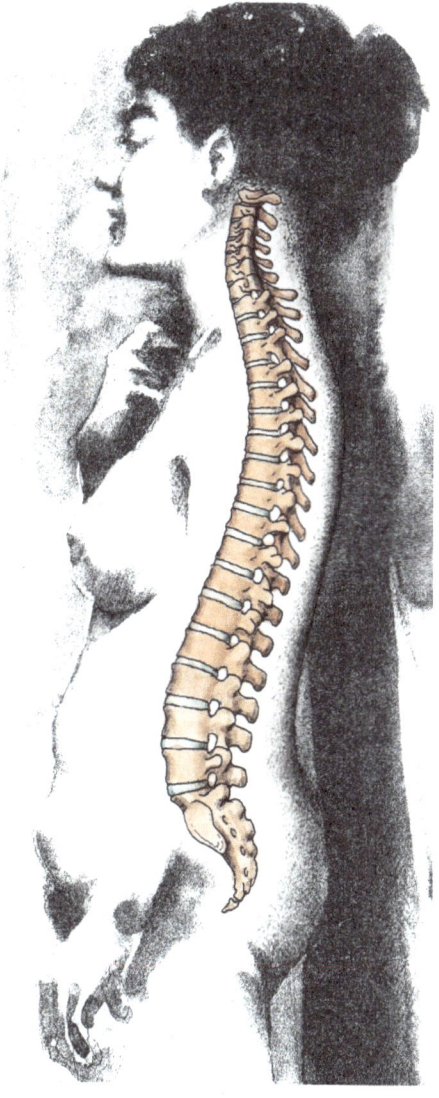

Side view of the 24 vertebra with their accompanying intravertebral discs atop the sacrum and coccyx, make up the vertebral column.

# The Sacrum and Coccyx

The Spinal, or Vertebral Column, announces its structure to the artists by the dimples running up the middle of the back. The sacrum, sitting at the base of this column will present a flat area with a dimple on each side. The pelvis, supporting the abdominal organs, has a ridge or crest encircling the lower abdomen, back to front. In front, these upper ridges end with a prominent spine called the anterior iliac spine. It is visible in most people and orients the direction of the pelvis.

The vertebral spinal column is composed of 24 vertebra, a sacrum, and coccyx. The sacrum is the evolutionary result of 5 segments fusing into one solid bone, acting as a base for the spinal column. The coccyx is a small vestigial final segment appended to the sacrum. The column has several front to back curves that help us in standing erect and aids in maintaining our balance. It is often beset by maladies, many of which are the result of a sedentary life style. The column begins by curving forward under the head, then curves back at the thorax to help provide enough space for our heart and lungs. (These curves are most likely evolutionary developments acquired as we started standing erect). And these curves can contribute to back problems. In particular, the Sacro-iliac Joint, at the base of the spine, with its acute curve, is often the cause of an aching back.

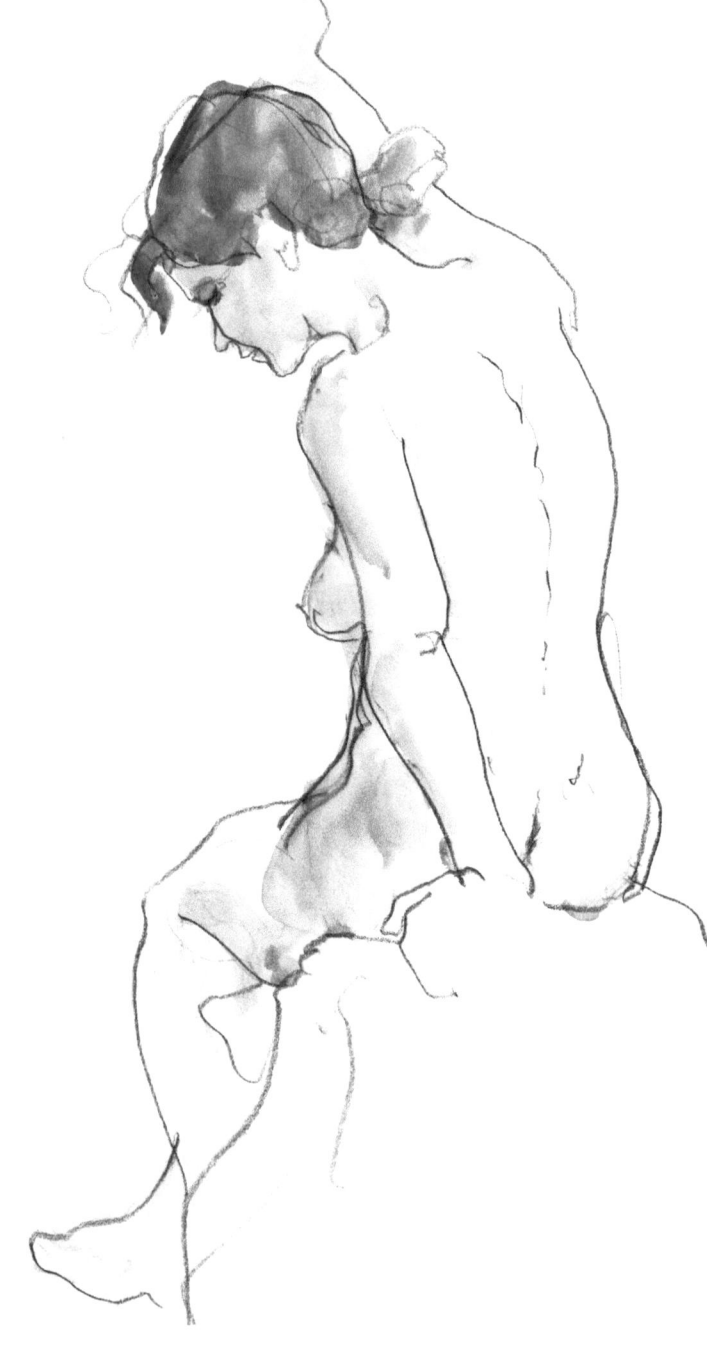

# The Female Hip

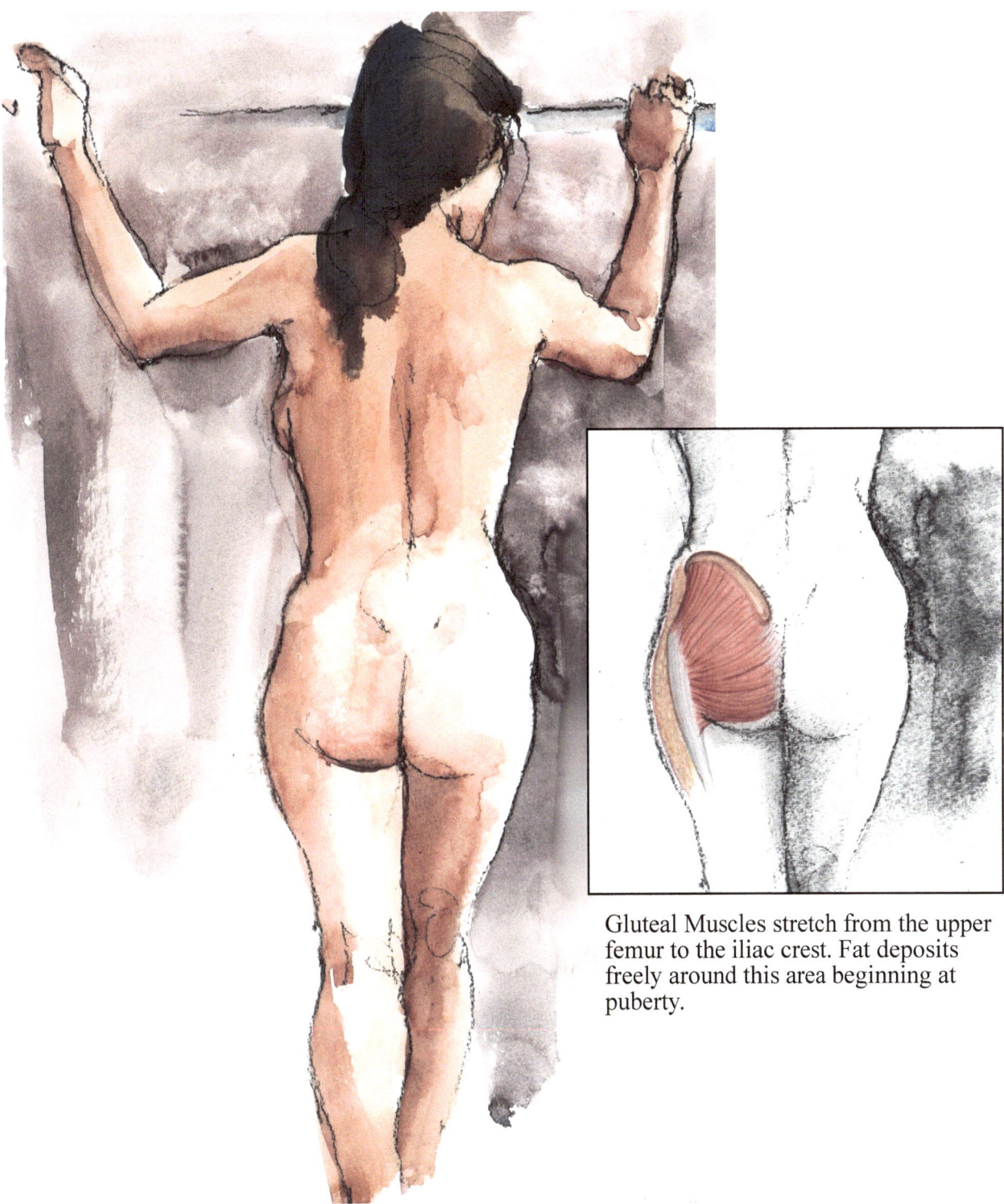

Gluteal Muscles stretch from the upper femur to the iliac crest. Fat deposits freely around this area beginning at puberty.

Post-pubertal fat defines the female form.

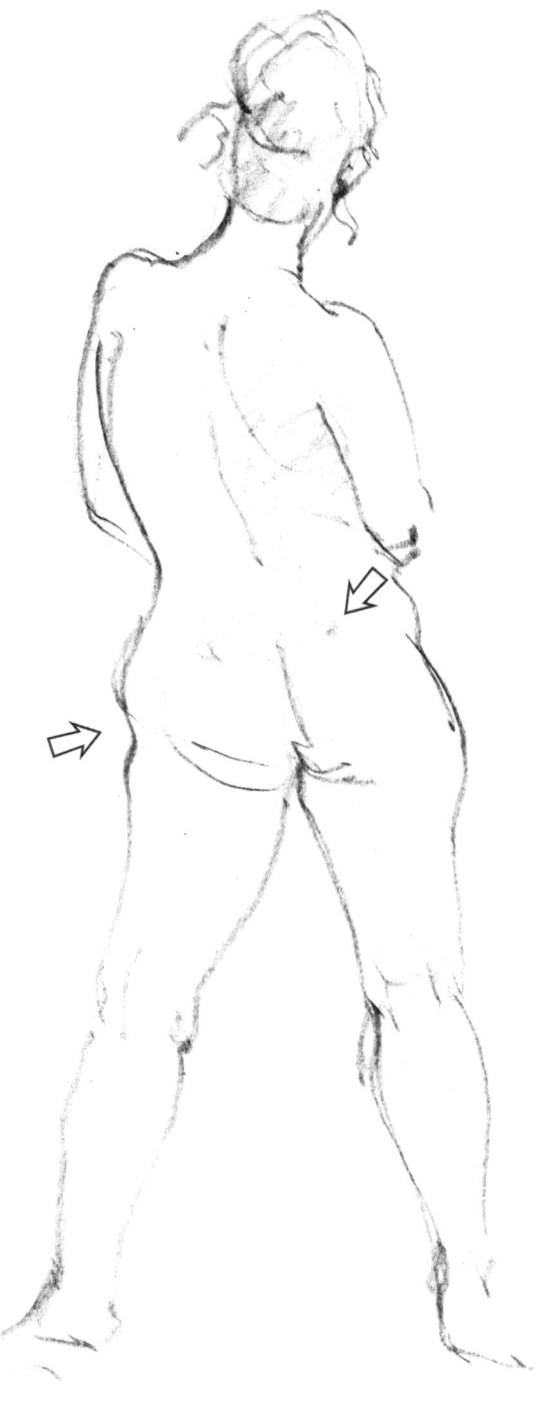

At puberty, fat begins to build up in the hip area of the average female. Hormones drive this deposition as it may have had an advantage for fat storage in pregnancy.

The depression, (lower arrow) so characteristic of the female hip, is caused by fat deposition around, but not at the place where the hip muscles (Gluteal Maximus and Minimus) attach at the upper part of the femur. The dimples (upper arrow) on either side at the base of the spine indicate the position of the sacrum.

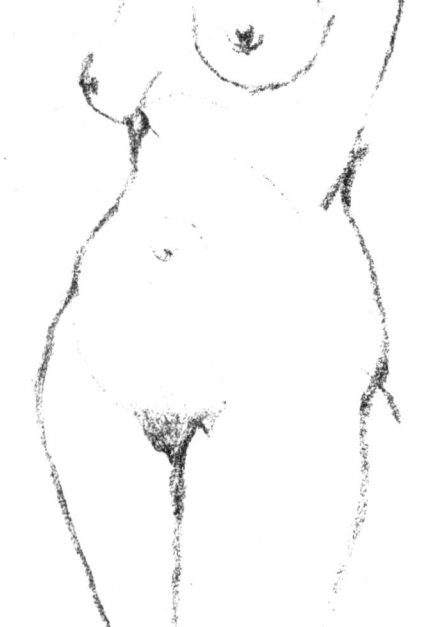

Quick sketches showing the characteristic dimple over the head of the femur.

# The Pelvis

The word pelvis is Latin for basin, and it is, indeed, basin shaped. The pelvis supports the abdominal organs, and in the female, it is usually large enough to coddle and carry a baby to full term, with an outlet large enough to then let the baby, when it is ready, move into this world. A woman's pelvis is usually wider than the male for the contingency of pregnancy. The anterior superior iliac spines (indicated) act as anchors for the sartorius muscle. The Sartorius and the oblique muscles of the abdomen blend into an aponeurosis, a fibrous sheath that encompasses the rectus abdominus, the so called six-pack of the muscle men.

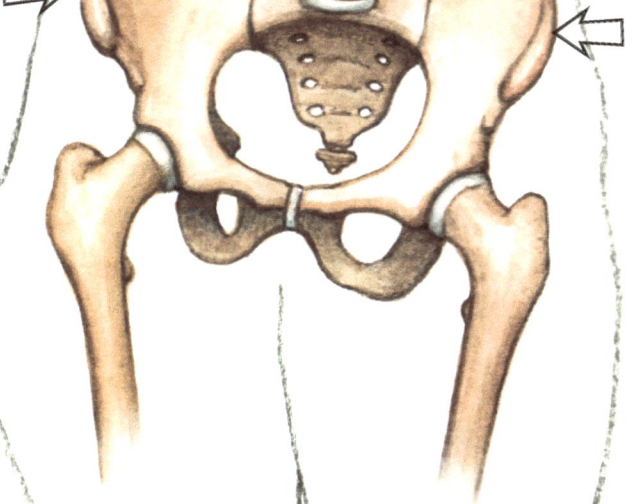

The pelvis, in position, with the Anterior Superior Iliac Spines indicated.

# The Female Pelvis

The upper legs of men and women are angled differently because of the wider pelvis in the female and the narrower, more upright pelvis in the male. The female pelvis is genetically equipped to carry a baby. It has a more bowl-like shape and has a wider inner pelvis opening to facilitate the passage of a full term fetus at birth.

Female Q angle < 17°

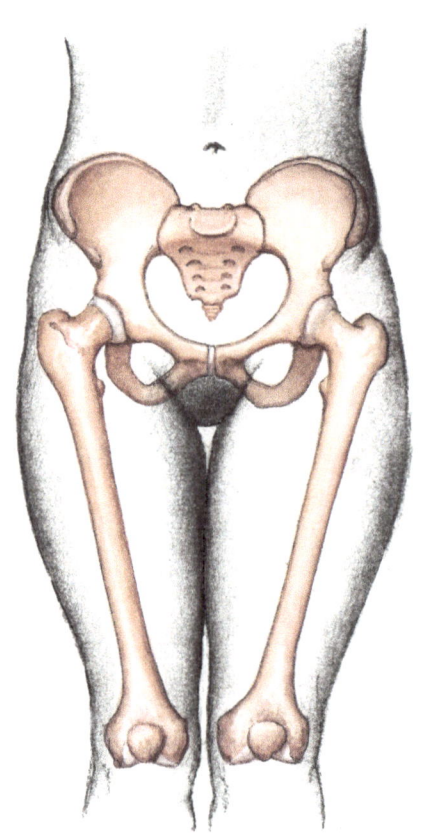

Female Pelvis

This wider female pelvis means that the upper leg bone, the femur, heads towards the lower leg at a greater angle than in the male. This angle is referred to as the "Q" angle. The average "Q" angle for the female is 17° or less and for the male it is 14° or less. The lower leg with its two major bones, the tibia and fibula, is normally vertical in both sexes. While the shape and width of the pelvis is generally greater in women, remember that the range for these anatomical features can vary greatly.

# The Male Pelvis
## Genetics is Destiny

Female track stars usually will be found to have narrower pelvises than the average woman, as this is a big advantage for speed. Their legs travel in a more vertical range, resulting in little wasted motion. While the male and female differences in form should be obvious to the art student, it is good to remember the anatomical reason behind these differences. Embryology research has shown that the differences in the male and female pelvis are determined as early as the 4th prenatal month. Indeed, genetics is destiny.

It was fun to see some recently constructed male and female robots on a TV news program. And sure enough, the female robot was built with a wider pelvis than the male. It's an indication of how people will immediately recognize sex differences without knowing why.

Male Q angle < 14°

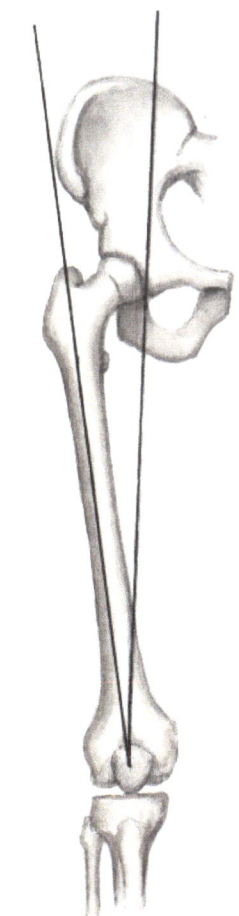

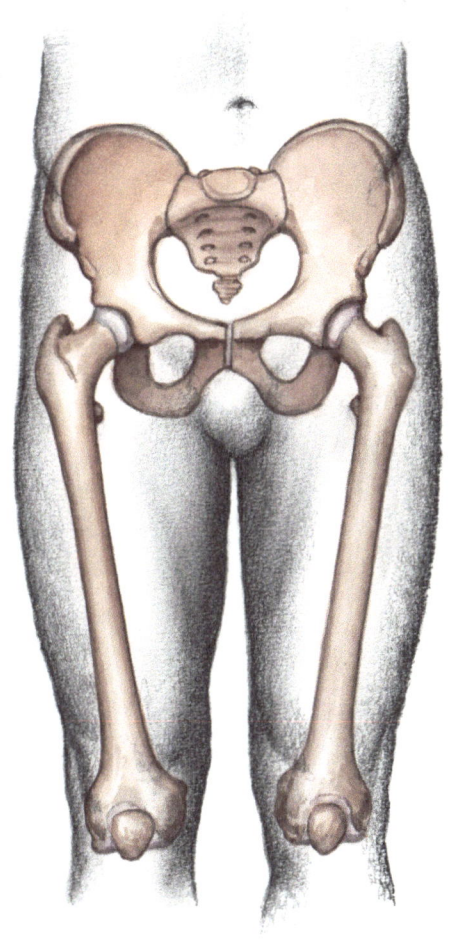

Male Pelvis

# Leg Muscles

The quadriceps muscles form the major muscle mass on the front of the upper leg and the hamstrings constitute the major muscle mass on the back. These are the two main groups of muscles on the thigh. The femur runs through the upper leg, more or less in the middle of these leg muscles.

On the lower leg most of the muscle mass is on the back, forming the calf muscles. This makes the lower leg look like it is positioned further back than the upper leg. Indeed the tibia, the main support for the lower leg, is just below the skin in the front (called the shin bone in popular parlance), while the femur is deep within all the upper leg muscles. The patella, protecting the knee joint, is a sesamoid bone. Sesamoid bones, by definition, are bones embedded in tendons. In this case the patella provides a smooth surface for the Quadricepts Tendon, as it slides over the knee joint, making flexion easier and more powerful. There are many other smaller muscle groups involved in the leg but their names and function add more complexity than clarity to our pursuit.

In drawing the leg from the side, note the structural asymmetry. It is essential to a true depiction while reflecting major leg muscle mass and functions.

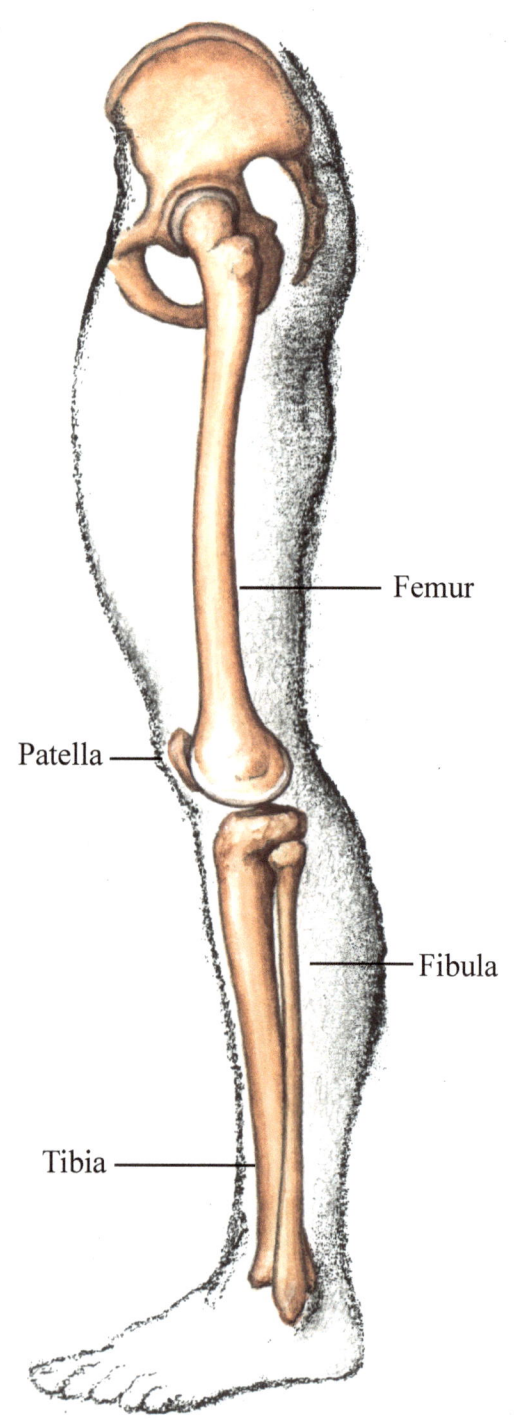

Femur

Patella

Fibula

Tibia

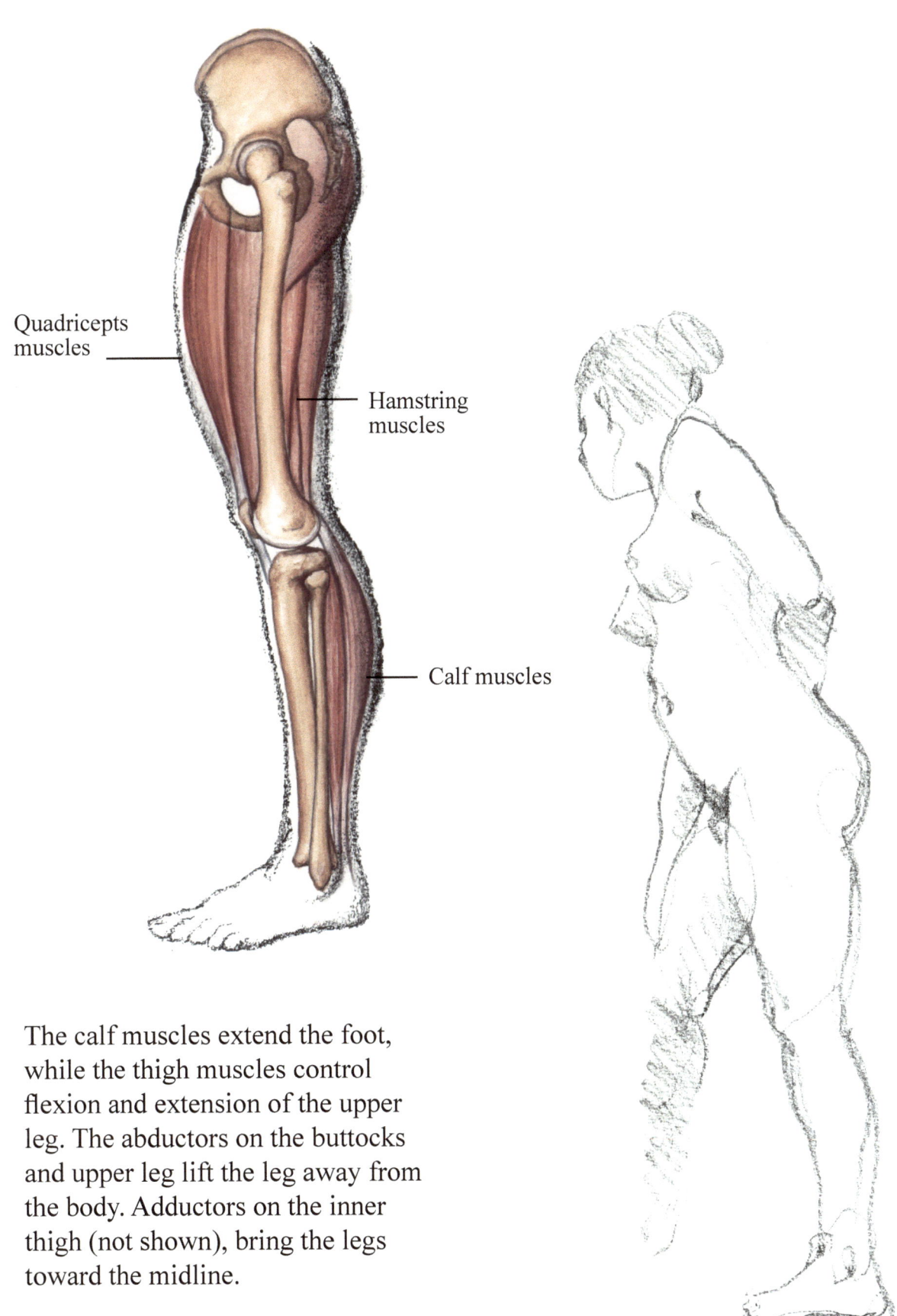

Quadricepts muscles

Hamstring muscles

Calf muscles

The calf muscles extend the foot, while the thigh muscles control flexion and extension of the upper leg. The abductors on the buttocks and upper leg lift the leg away from the body. Adductors on the inner thigh (not shown), bring the legs toward the midline.

# Sartorius Muscle

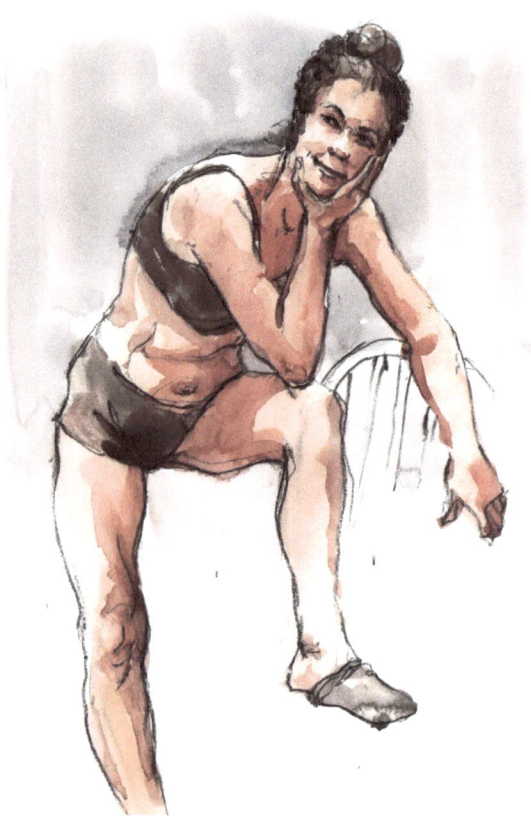

The Sartorius muscle is the longest muscle in the body and works as a flexor of the hip and leg. It gets its name from the Latin word for tailor because the tailors of old sat cross-legged while working at their trade (or so the story goes). This muscle supposedly grew more prominent from use as tailors were continually getting up and down while working.

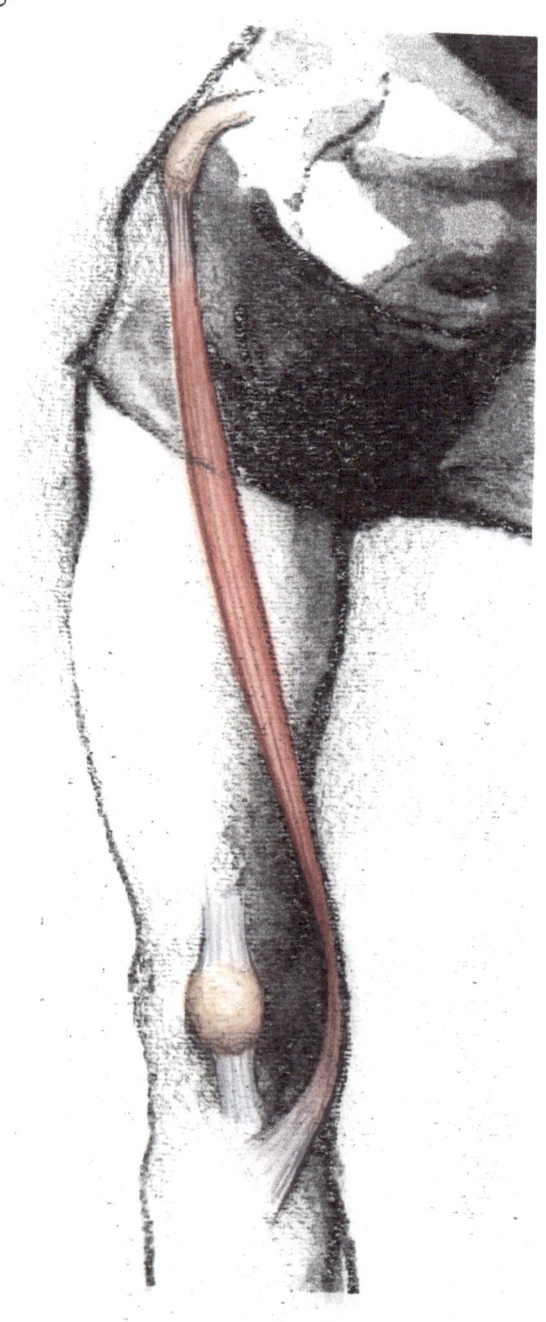

The muscle's path crosses both the hip joint and the knee, as it wraps itself around the upper leg to insert below, on the inside of the tibial bone, thus flexing both the hip and knee joint. It is a landmark worth searching out while sketching. It is easier to see in the male and best seen in thin models, but its path can be identified in almost everybody. It gives the upper leg character and its curved path will be recognized immediately because the muscle itself lies in an evident, smoothly curved groove.

In the anatomical, note how the muscle crosses both the hip and the knee joint.

# The Knee

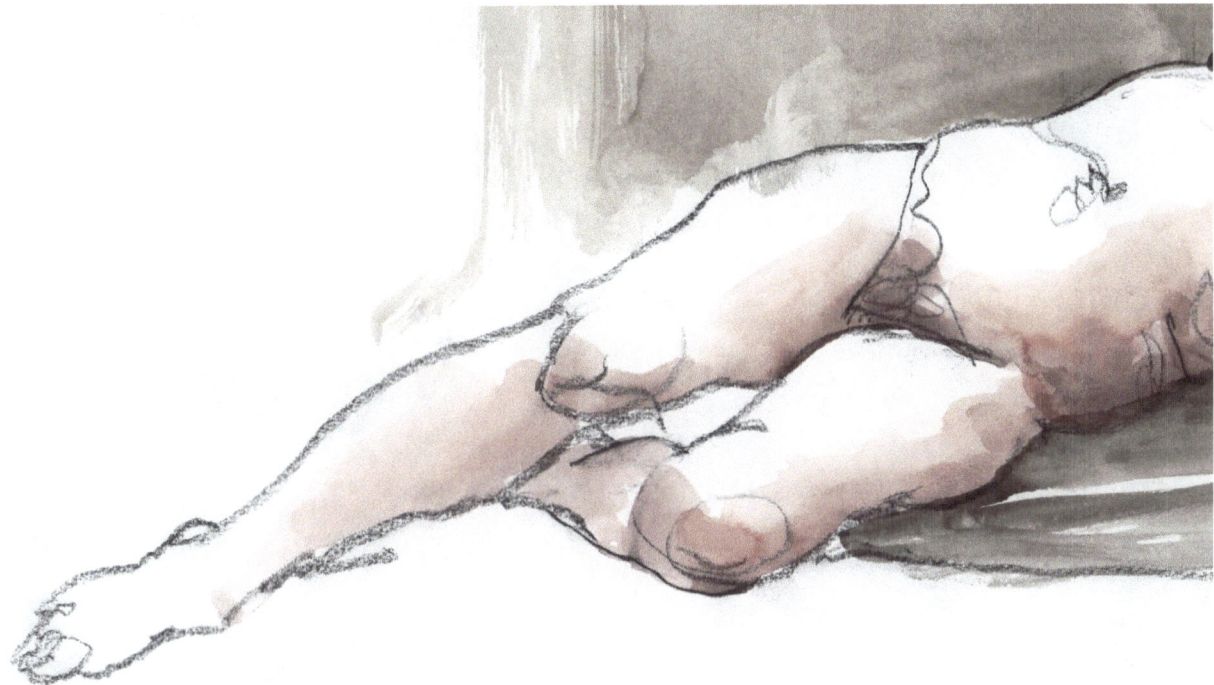

**P**ainting the knee gives artists more trouble than any other simple structure in the body. Ostensibly, a hinge joint, it is basically composed of the femur, tibia, and the patella. It is, in reality, much more complex than that. Some limited inward and outward rotation of the lower leg can be achieved as needed. This enables quick changes of direction.

In sports this can make the difference between success or failure on the field or in court games. In one's daily life, quick turns are essential in crowds and even when you are on a simple shopping trip.

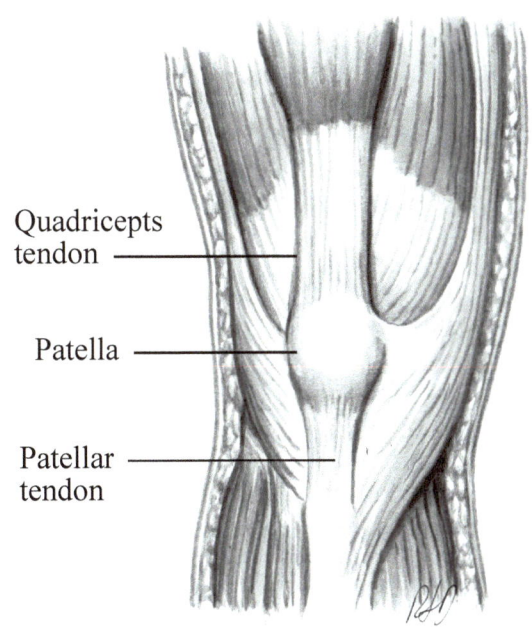

Quadricepts tendon

Patella

Patellar tendon

The knee joint is bounded by ligaments and tendons. They help keep the knee stable and anchor many of the leg muscles. The most prominent tendons are the patellar and quadricept tendons. The patella, or knee cap, is a sesamoid bone–defined as a bone within a tendon.

The Knee Joint is the largest and most visible of our sesamoids. It functions as an aid in extension of the lower leg. Our body contains several other sesamoids but they are very small and usually can be found under the big toe and sometimes within a thumb tendon.

Problems for the artist can develop as people gain fat. Women, in particular, can develop fatty bulges aroung the knee that often obscure the patella. Search out the patella, as it sits in front of the joint, for it defines the knee. It protects the joint proper and adds leverage to the action of the quadricepts muscle in knee extension.

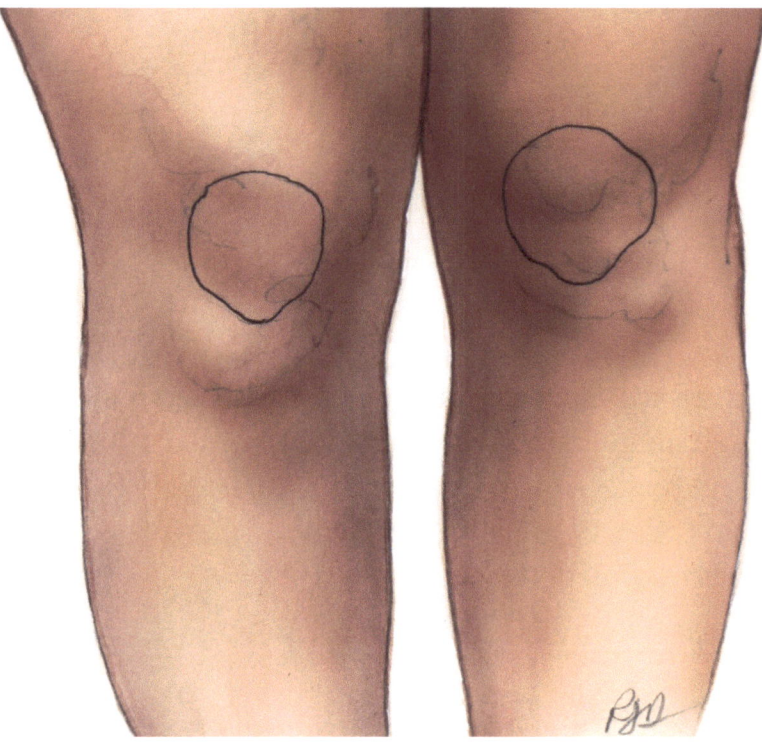

In the above drawing of a model's knees, you can see how fat pads obscure the patella. Although I have outlined the position of the patella, finding it under the fat pads can be difficult.

My anatomical illustration of the underlying knee structures on the previous page shows how extensive the tendons are in covering the knee and how the patella sits directly in front of the knee joint. As your model moves his or her leg, the patella usually becomes more apparent, especially when the leg is flexed. Any time the model is seated or squats down, the patella presents itself directly over the joint space. Look for it, it is a rest stop for your pencil – an important marker when drawing the leg.

# The Ankle

The ankle bones, when seen from the front, are asymmetrical. The Tibia and Fibula each end in what is called a malleolus, or bony projection, that helps form the upper limits of the ankle joint. The word is derived from the Latin for mallet, which is a fine description for its nobby shape. The outer bone, the fibula, with its malleolus, is always lower than the inner malleolus of the tibia. This strengthens and protects the ankle joint. Never draw them directly opposite each other. Drawing them correctly adds a lifelike quality to depictions of the lower leg.

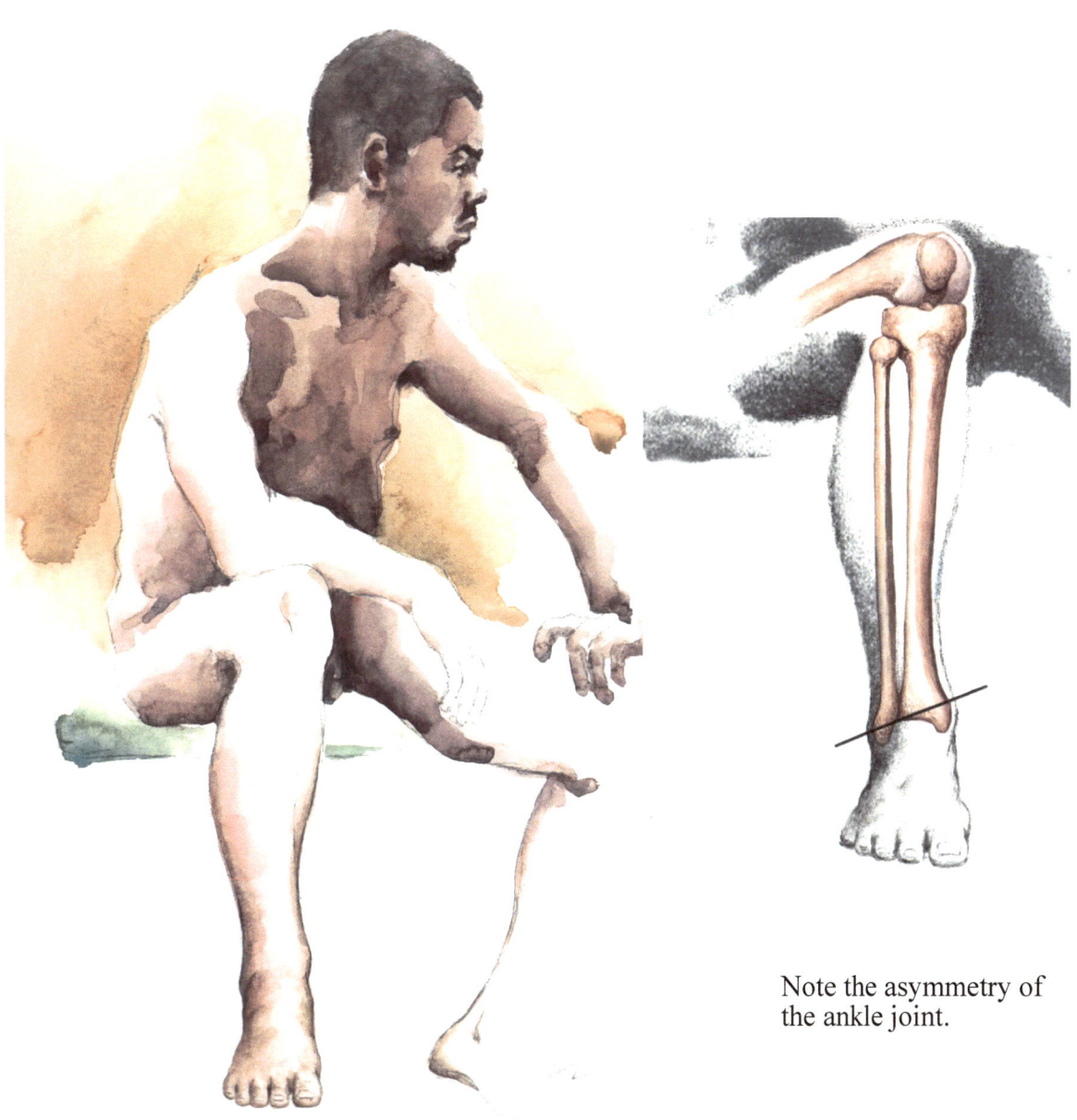

Note the asymmetry of the ankle joint.

# A Different Model

It's nice to be surprised when the model shows up. Different body types, different ages, their gender, clothed or unclothed, covered with tattoos, or plain-jane, they are all part of our world, and could be part of any paintings you may produce. Welcome them.

# The Pregnant Model

**O**ccasionally, I have been surprised to find that our model for the day is pregnant. What a joy. It represents a new challenge for the artist and a further test to one's powers of observation, to say nothing about the joy ahead for the future mother. Pregnancy increasingly affects a woman's center of gravity. There are many changes in store for the future mother, some obvious and some more subtle.

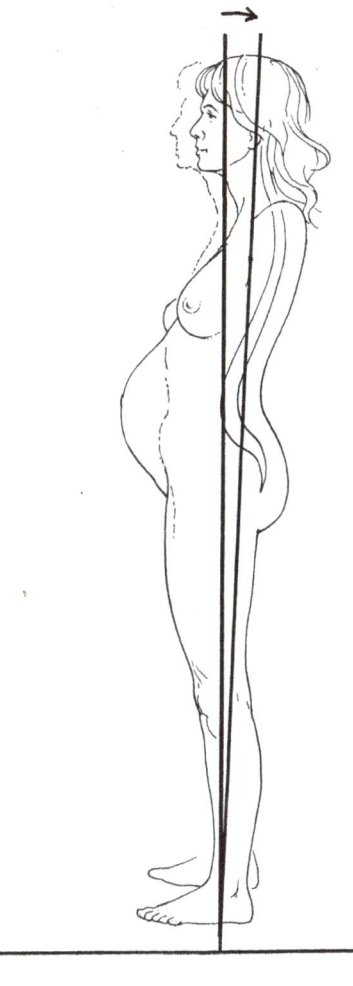

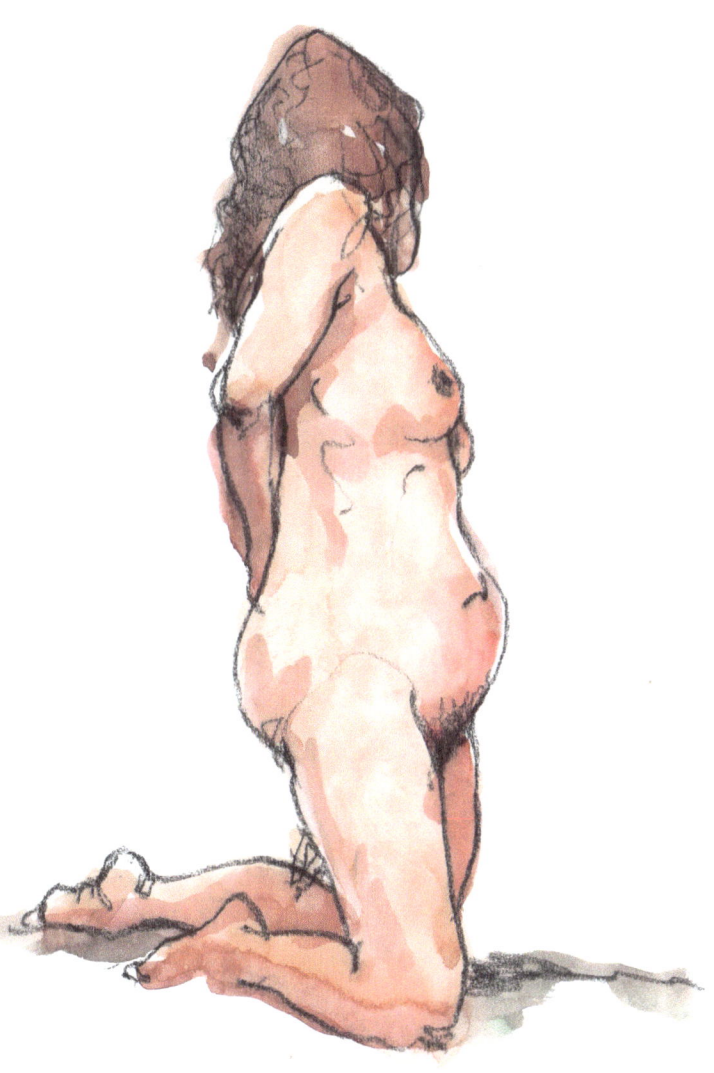

With a woman in the more advanced stages of pregnancy, you will easily notice her backwards lean when seen from the side. This is essentially a balancing move because of the forward weight of the fetus affecting her center of gravity.

By increasingly leaning backwards a pregnant woman can maintain her balance as she compensates for the weight of the growing baby.

Of course, the breasts are swelling as they get ready for nursing, and the milk glands increase in size. The nipple areaola darkens. Other changes, some more subtle, occur. One of the more unpleasant changes is the occasional swelling of the feet, as both the legs veins and lymph channels, coursing past the growing fetus, attempt to move blood and lymph back toward the heart.

Because of the increasing physical strain of pregnancy, be prepared for more sitting and lying poses. Energetic one or two minute poses can be too taxing on the model. A real treat for the artist would be for the new mother to come back one day, and pose with the baby!

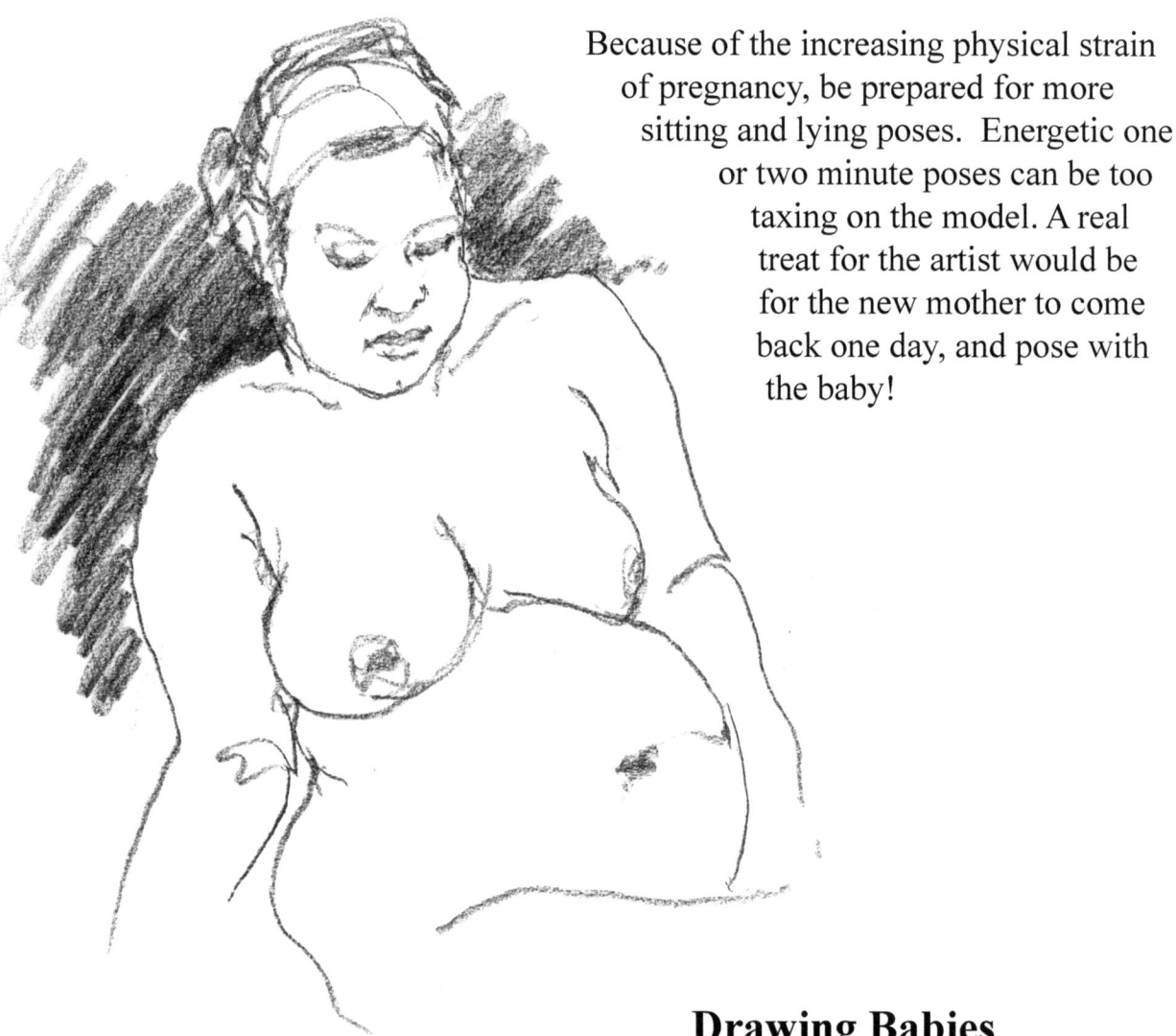

## Drawing Babies

**B**abies are born with their heads (and brains) in an advanced stage of development. As a result their heads often push the limits of the birth canal. While their heads, at birth, are as large as possible, their bodies are only about 5% of their eventual adult size. Their head will grow but not nearly as fast as their body will. At birth, babies are a little more than 4 heads in length. Our large heads are probably the result of evolutionary survival pressures. Big brains win!

In the Gothic period painters and sculptors often began depicting children. Understandably, the baby Jesus was very popular. The Christ child, in their depictions of the Madonna and Child, was proportioned as a small adult, including the head to body size relationship. Even at the dawn of the Renaissance in the 1300's, artists such as Giotto, Duccio and Cimabue, reaching up to Bellini in 1460 and Crivelli in 1480, were still depicting the Christ Child in ways that are surprising to the modern eye. They simply painted the child with what they thought were the correct proportions and not what was truly staring them in the face everday. This points to the value of observation, and how difficult observing reality can be. As children grow their bodies grow faster than their heads until, in their early 20s, they reach fully grown proportions, with their bones no longer adding new height and breadth.

I have written about the importance of observation in drawing, and eschewing the use of measurements and scales of various kinds to help proportion the figure. If the early paintiers had used their observational skills they would have seen their mistake. Of course, if it was easy to see our mistakes, we would all be better artists.

Sketch of newborn with the umbilical cord still attached.

47

# Capturing a Likeness

So many portraits are painted that are nothing but painted photographs. No insight is evident into the personality of the person portrayed. It is much like so many of the mansions being built in upscale communities all over America. The architect does not really know the people for whom he is designing the house. By using the Procrustes Bed approach every client gets the same house. They are made to fit the house, not the other way around. That same approach is evident in too many portrait artists work. You have got to know your client well to paint him well. If you go on to portraiture work spend time getting to know your client. For a portrait to be effective it must reflect that person's personality. James Balestrieri says,

*"A great portrait is a balancing act between capturing a likeness and revealing inner character, between fidelity to appearance – verisimilitude – and exposing the sitter's inner light…"* [3]

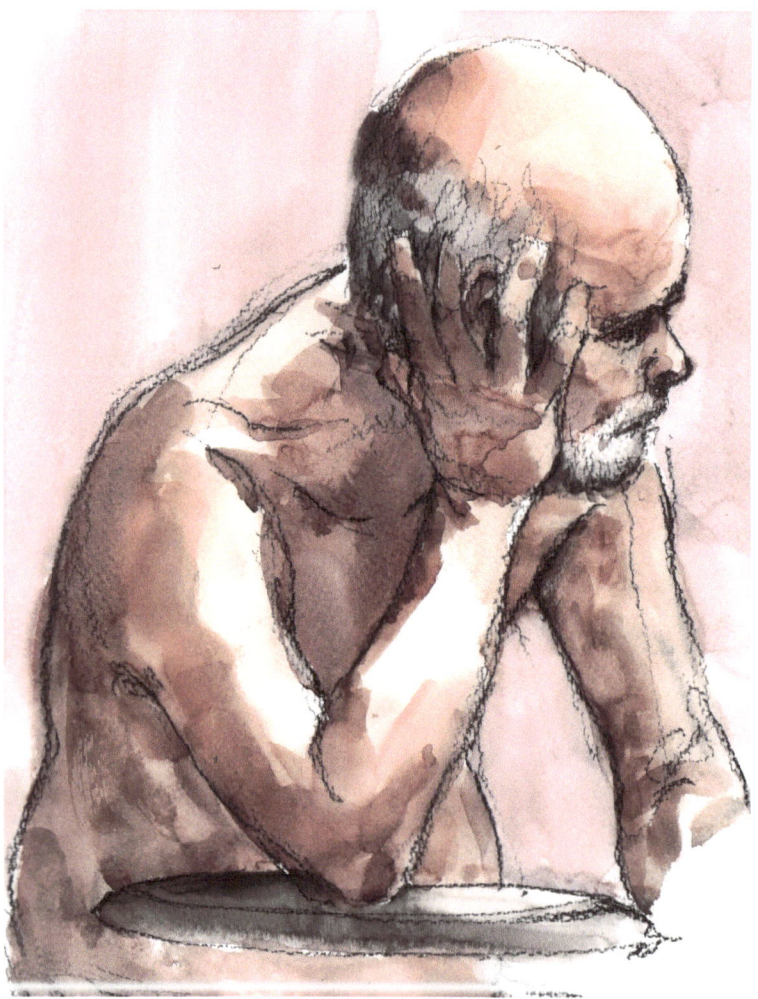

A good portrait artist tries to capture the unique flame that burns in each of us. Life Class is a good place to practice working toward a likeness. Try capturing the tilt of the head, the unruly hair, or the frown lines and the wrinkles that are unique to the model.

Make it part of the same approach you use on your gesture or contour drawings. Make it your sketch.

3. Antique & Arts Weekly (March 18, 2016) Van Dyke: The Anatomy of Portraiture. p.1

Roberta Smith of the *New York Times* wrote of the Flemish artist Anthony Van Dyke's approach to portrait painting:

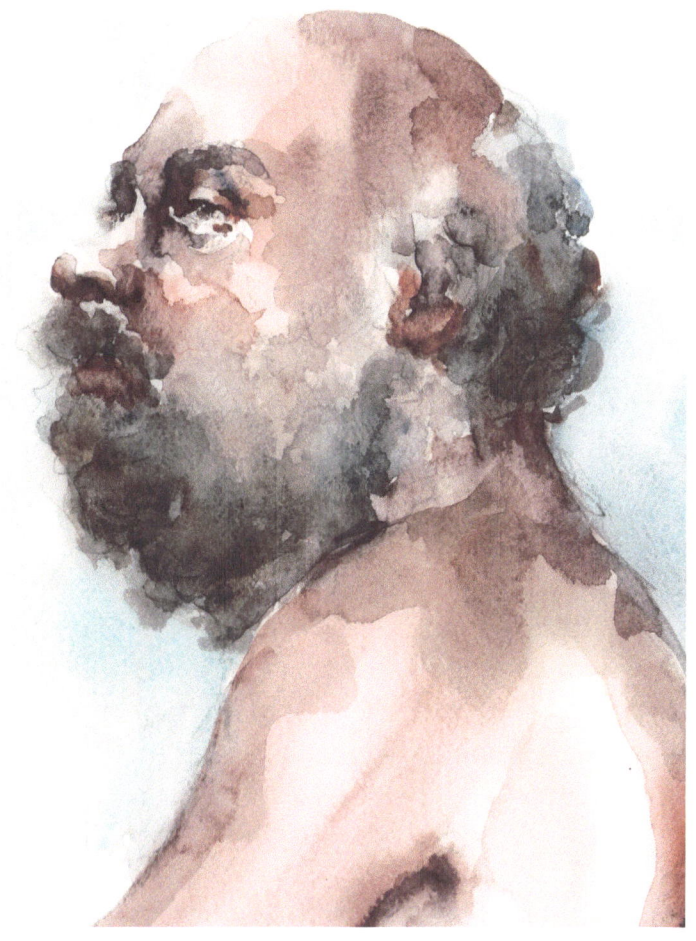

***"The paintings are complimented… by an extraordinary array of drawings that reflect an artist able to indicate the pose, clothing and facial expression of a portrait in a few quick strokes of black chalk."*** [4]

I'll take a few quick, telling strokes, any time.

Several years ago Bernard Denvir produced a small book in which he reproduced all of the known Vincent Van Gogh's self portraits. They are reproduced chronologically. One of his very first portraits was sketched in 1885 and a later portrait is dated 1887. The difference is stark. The first self portrait gives no hint of the genius to soon emerge. The competence in the later work is so evident that one must ask – did he learn to draw in that short period of a year and one half, or did he learn how to really observe what he was looking at? Just seeing better, seeing more, I believe leads to better drawing. Indeed it may be the real benefit of an art class- any art class. Van Gogh, in one of his letters to his brother Theo writes,

***"I want to paint men and women with that something of the eternal which the halo used to symbolize, and which we seek to convey..."*** [5]

Would that he lived beyond his 38 years.

4. Robert Smith. New York Times – Weekend Arts. Friday, March 11, 2016
5. Van Gogh wrote to his brother Theo, on September 3, 1888

Quick sketching of just a model's face is often a good exercise, particulary, during short drawing sessions. Sometimes the model will take a pose that you will find is of little interest to you. That gives you an opportunity to sketch his or her face or, maybe, your fellow artists. Many of my better sketches are of my classmates. It is also good training for a future sketching trip to outdoor market places, the subway, or train stations.

Biologists at Caltech have discovered small groups of facial recognition neurons in the brain that respond and recognize a face in a few thousandths of a second. This almost instant recognition was probably extremely important in identifying members of one's own social group, ensuring their survival in difficult times. These neurons may measure small deviations from an "average" face for this recognition.

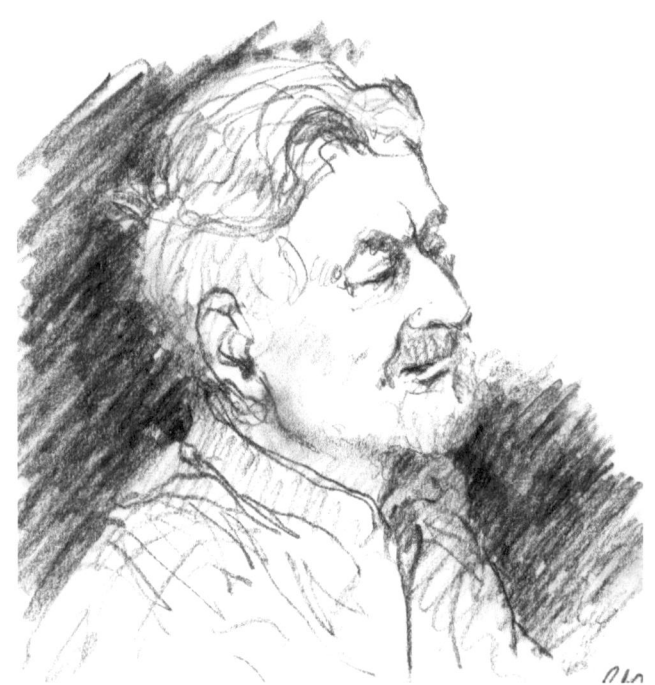

Four consecutive 1 minute poses

Fellow classmate

Considering that we remember thousands of faces, each one only a little different than the next, emphasizes just how a subtle difference can make each face unique. Think what that means for the portrait artist. We have to look for those subtle differences. They can be small, but essential to an individual's personality. How someone holds their head, the flicker of a smile, raising an eyebrow, or a small asymmetry, may be all it takes to capture a person in paint. It is no wonder why there are so few truly great portrait artists.[6]

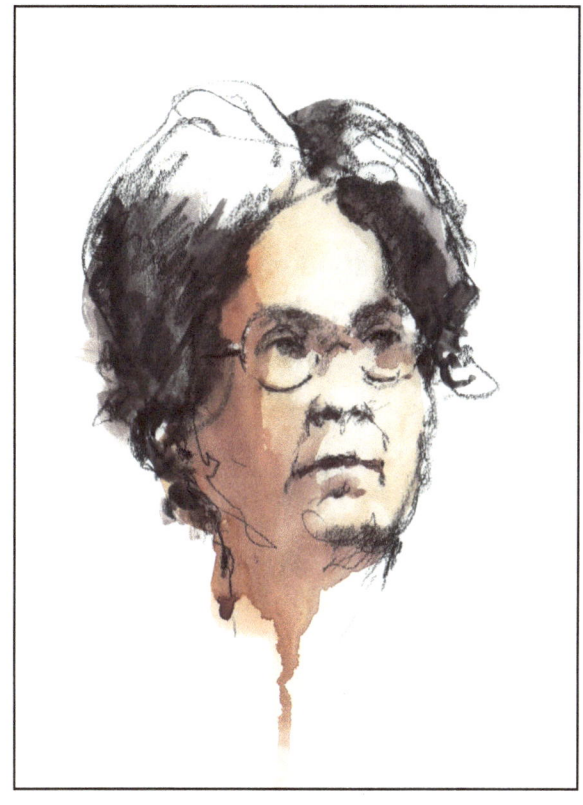

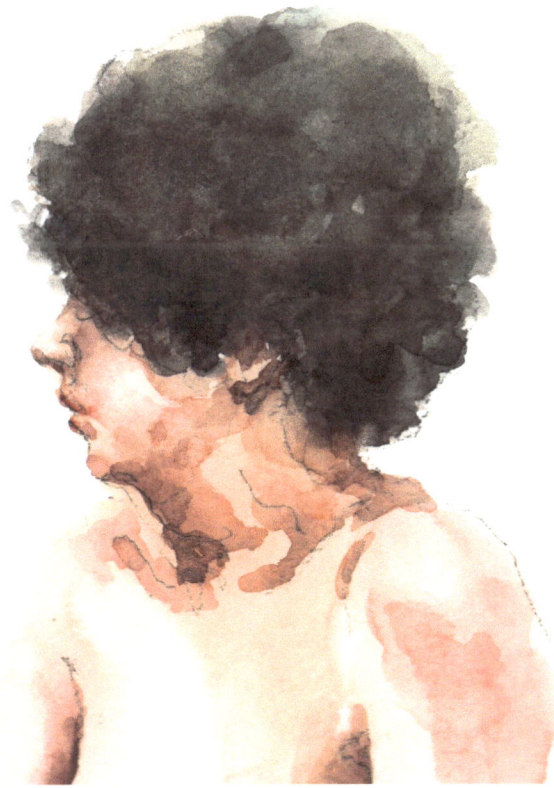

Degas' approach to portraiture is a worthwhile challenge to us all.

*'.... depict people in familiar and typical attitudes, above all to give to their faces the same choice of expression as one gives to their bodies.'* [7]

Sometimes a quick sketch can capture more of the personality of a model than all the careful drawing and redrawing you can ever do. Is it what the artist leaves out? Is it the result of concentrating on their key features? I think we are capable of more than we realize if only we just let our inner artist take over.

6. The New York Times, Science Times section, June 6, 2017
7. Notebooks of Edgar Degas. Editor: Theodore Reff 1976

I am reminded of Cezanne's portraits and in particular of one well known exchange recorded in Ambroise Vollard's book, "Cezanne's Studio." Cezanne was painting a portrait of Vollard, who moved his body during the sitting. "Unfortunate man! You must be quiet as a apple - an apple that never moves." Do I have to tell you again you must sit like an apple? "Besides when one poses one must be quiet." It exemplifies the problem of portraiture. The personality, that spark of individuality, slowly drains from the sitter as the sessions lengthen. It is almost inevitable. Cezanne's, "The Card Players" is a perfect example of the problem. Julian Barnes[8] says that "Cezanne's portraits are all still-lives. Those card players bent over their table are never actually going to play a card or take a trick...."

The way Frans Hals managed to capture the spontaniety of his sitters made his portraits unforgettable. Was it his preparation, his personality, his palette, or all of these, plus something intangible?

The story of Yousuf Karsh of Canada (1908-2002), one of the greatest portrait photographers of the 20th century, and his encounter with Winston Churchill, is an example of one way to solve the problem. Churchill didn't want to sit for a photograph and did so reluctantly. He sat down with that ever present cigar in his mouth and when asked to remove it, refused. Karsh pretending to take a light meter reading near his subject, snatched the cigar from Churchill's mouth as he clicked the shutter on his camera. Churchill's pugnacious, bulldog expression, was captured for eternity.

The difficulty of capturing any personality in paint or on film is easily understood. How does one capture the essence of an individual and freeze it in paint? Interminable sittings are no guarantee of success –often just the opposite. My only advice is to get to know your sitter well enough to see the light in their eyes and the bounce in their step. Do not force them to sit like an apple. Look for that halo!

8. Julian Barnes. Keeping an Eye Open. Alfred Knopf, New York 2015

# The View from the Model Stand

In interviewing models for this book it is evident that all models are different and they all look at their job differently. Some, recognizing the demands of the profession, take it very seriously, while others simply consider it a way to earn a living. The serious ones usually make the session more interesting and satisfying for both the artists and the model.

# The View from the Model Stand

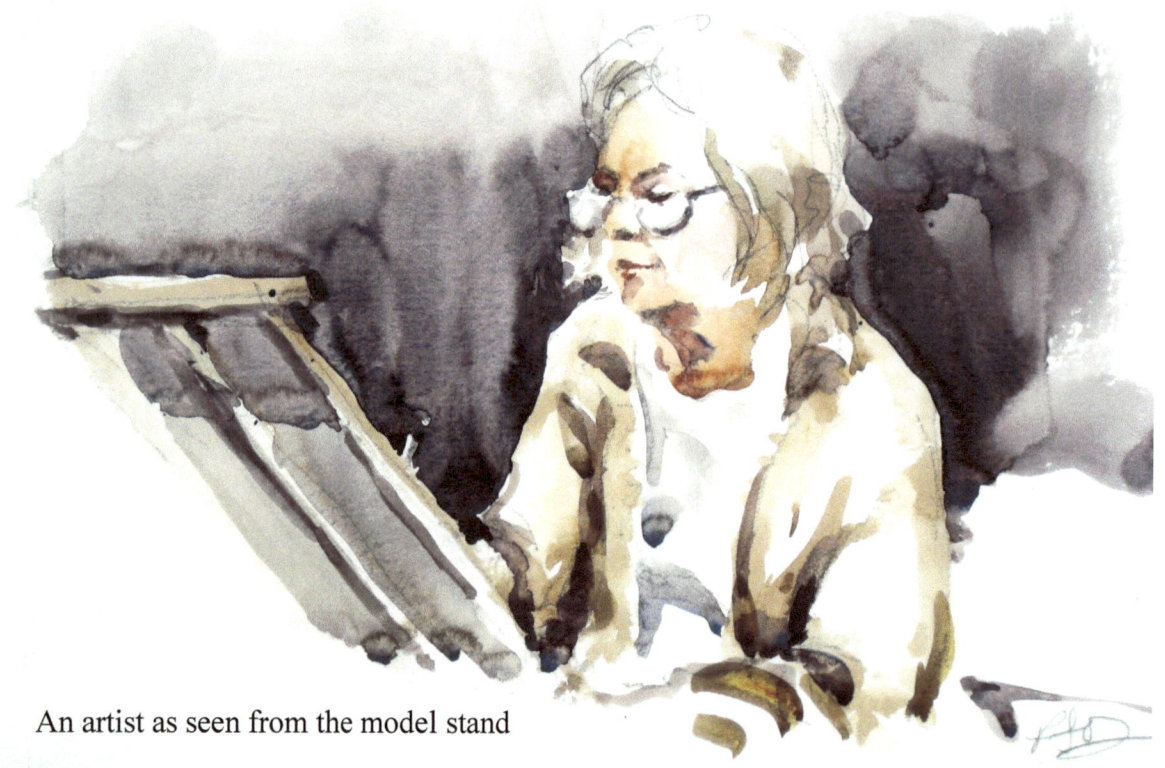

An artist as seen from the model stand

The model's space should be inviolate. We mostly draw from a table, an easel, or use the back of a chair to support a pad, all at some remove from the model stand. One should never venture into the model's space while they are working. During rest periods some models express interest in what, and how well, the artists are drawing. At these times a model, now robed, will have an opportunity to look at the artists' work. Some never do. Is it all just about getting paid to pose naked? Is there no interest in the product that they, the model for that product, are so instrumental in producing? Could they learn something about modeling if they looked at what the artists are producing? Of course they could.

## Using her body as a tool

A good model should approach each modeling session with three things in mind. One, tell a story; two, express a feeling; and three, use the model platform space in an interesting way. The effective use of the space that the model inhabits is crucial for the life class artists if they are to achieve a good sketch or painting. Not all poses look great from every side of the room. Knowing this, the model must change her focus during the session, paying attention to every artist's workspace.

It is a complimentary relationship with both the artist and the model making an investment in the results. Some models take an interest in each artist's work because they want to see if their poses have proven successful. A good model must be aware of the value of the controppostal pose. Contropposto is a Greek word for an assymetrical arrangement of arms and legs contrasting with those of the hips and legs, as opposed to taking a more static, balanced pose. By extension, it can be applied to any pose where the hips and legs are turned in a different direction from the shoulders and head. These twists and thrusts give added interest to a figure drawing.

Too many models take no interest in what the artists are producing. A good model makes sure that everyone in the class has an opportunity to draw a prime view. This means facing a different part of the room with each pose. It means the model must think in 3-dimensional terms with his or her body and the relationship between the model and the place of each student in the class.

One of my favorite models starts her session clothed, and her initial one and two minute poses are the steps she takes in undressing. This activity allows for an interesting series of stop-action poses full of bending, pulling off a garment, taking off boots or socks, etc.

There is nothing suggestive about this common daily act, one we all go through every day. Pulling off a boot on a cold winter day makes the word "pose" almost inappropriate. This is the real world approach to a modeling session, while injecting each pose with meaningful action.

5 minute pose

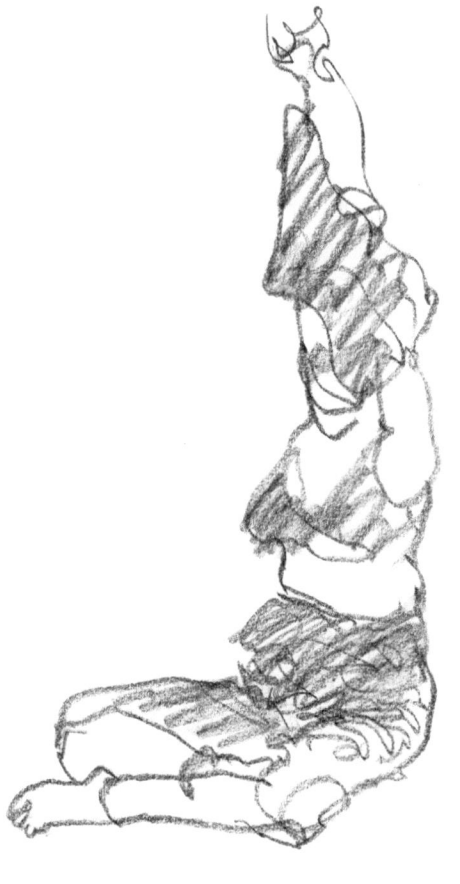

Rodin had models in his studio at all times and sketched whenever he saw an action that impressed him. So many good, sketch-worthy poses, are drawn from common everyday activities.

One minute poses

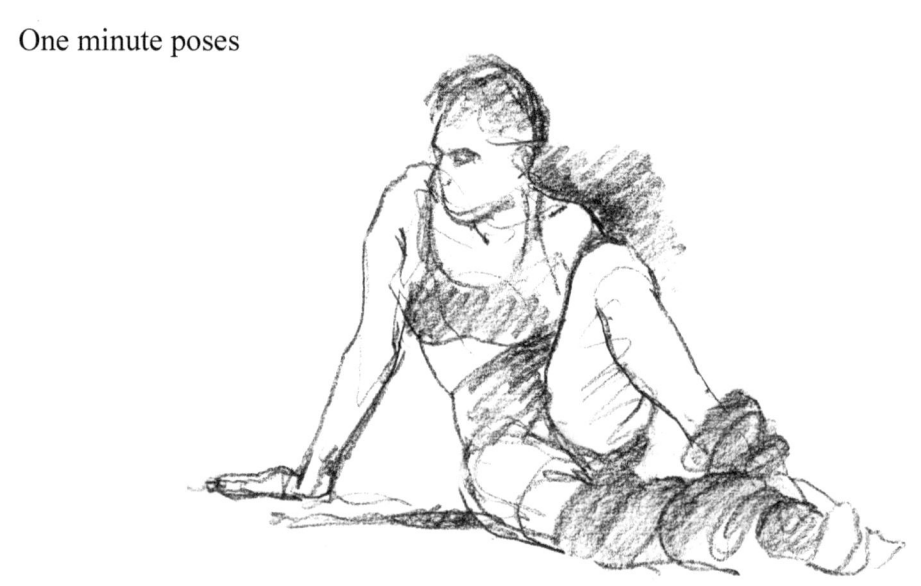

One minute poses

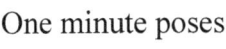

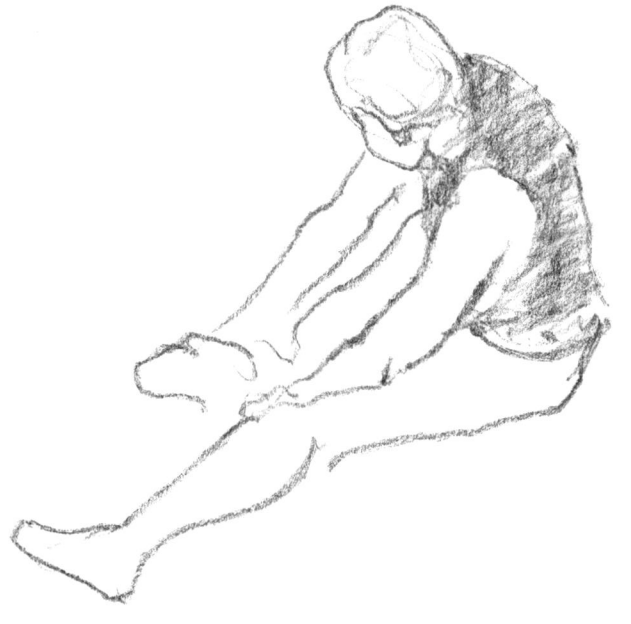

A prop or piece of equipment can inspire a series of interesting poses. A hoop, a baseball bat, or even a pole can trigger interesting action. Degas found a rich treasure for his work sketching a model in the act of bathing.

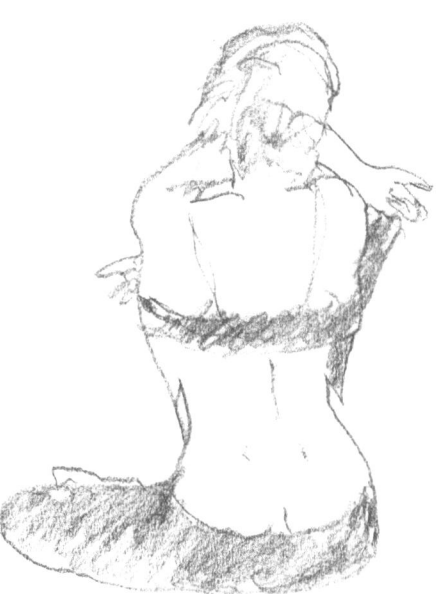

While a bathtub may be out of place in a life class, a towel, a scarf, or a beach ball can act as a catalyst for a worthwhile drawing session.

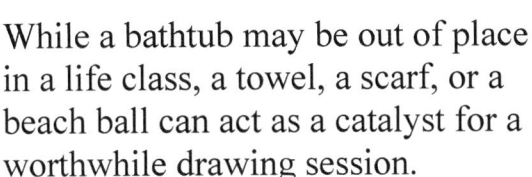

# All nude, all day?

Not every pose has to be in the nude. On a cold January day it can be a relief, and fun for the class, to paint a model wearing a leotard or with a shawl wrapped over her shoulders. It can't be much fun to pose nude in a drafty studio.

One of my favorite figure studies is "Nude in a Fur Coat" (see: The Longer Pose section). Some models, more modest than most, will want to cover their genital area. A little "G" string or colored panties might be worn in class. It matters little.

I can remember the days when male models wore an athletic supporter.

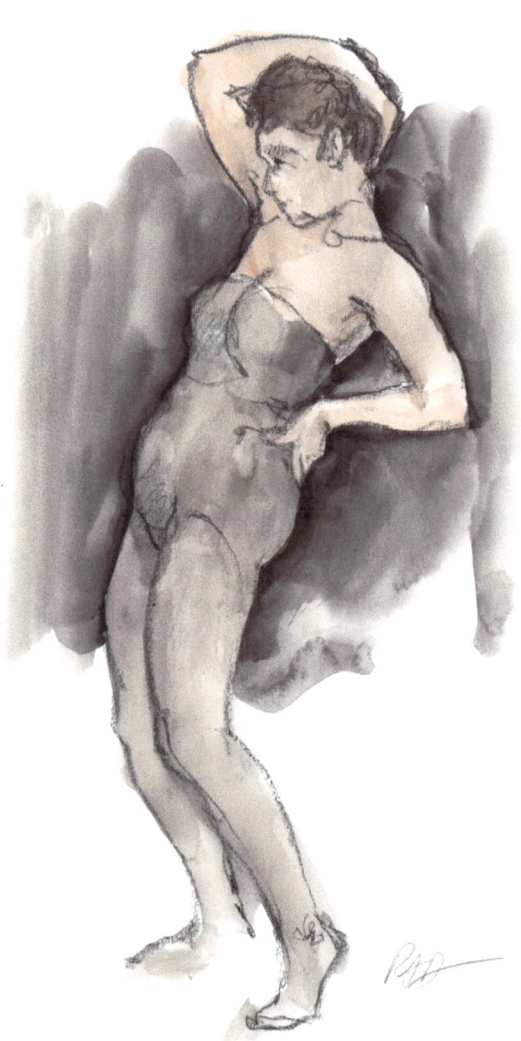

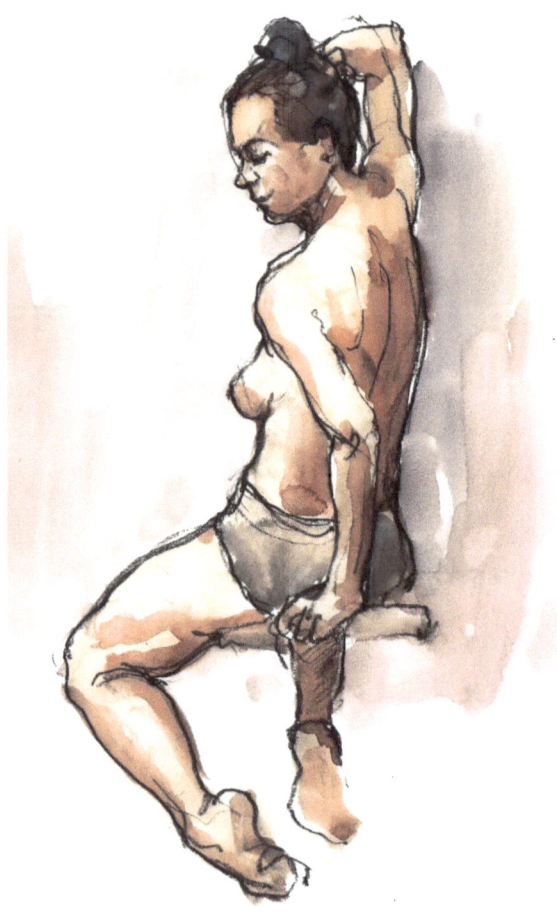

Fortunately, that sense of modesty is long gone.

58

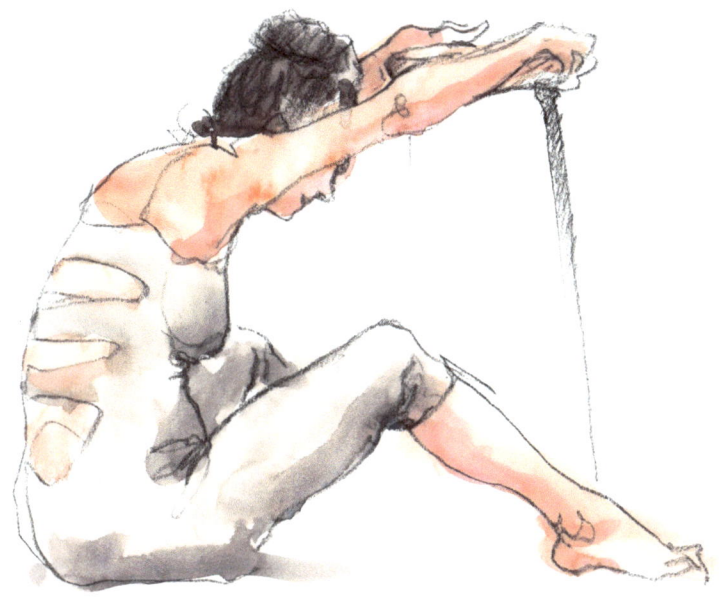

This model was wearing a ladderback leotard. Garb such as this can cause your eye to lose command of the subtle curves of the back. It's hard to disregard unusual attire but persistence pays off.

Occasionally, a model, more modest than most, will insist on posing in a two-piece bathing suit. The modeling world is an unorganized work place and variety is common. It's never hum-drum in life class.

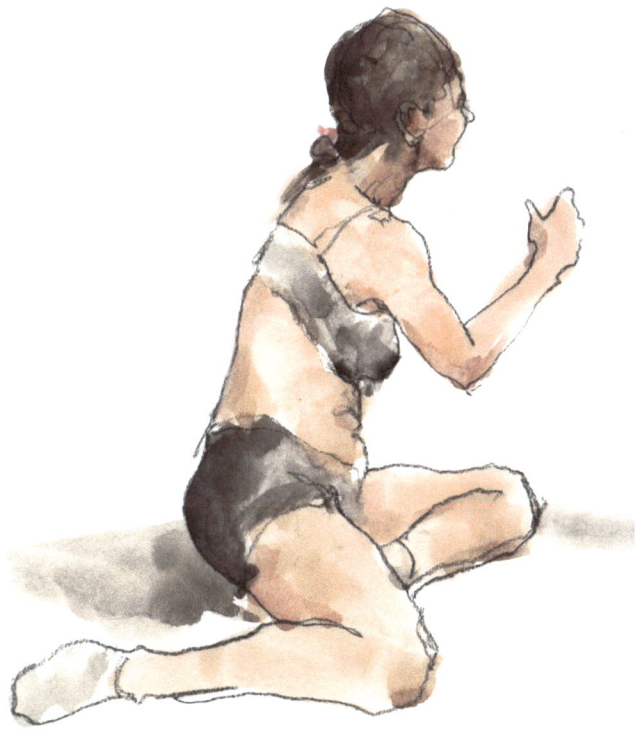

# The Male Model

The male model seems to be an endangered species. The average art class can expect to have a female model a high percentage of the time. This gender disparity in art classes is so prevalent that it was the subject of an op-ed piece in the New York Times. The writer, a man who was looking at art modeling to make a few extra dollars, was warmly welcomed to an art class even though he had no experience modeling. It made for an interesting and amusing story. Back in the 19th century the art academy models were all men. That has certainly changed. I have had a fellow artist tell me that she has trouble drawing men because she has so little experience working with a male figure.

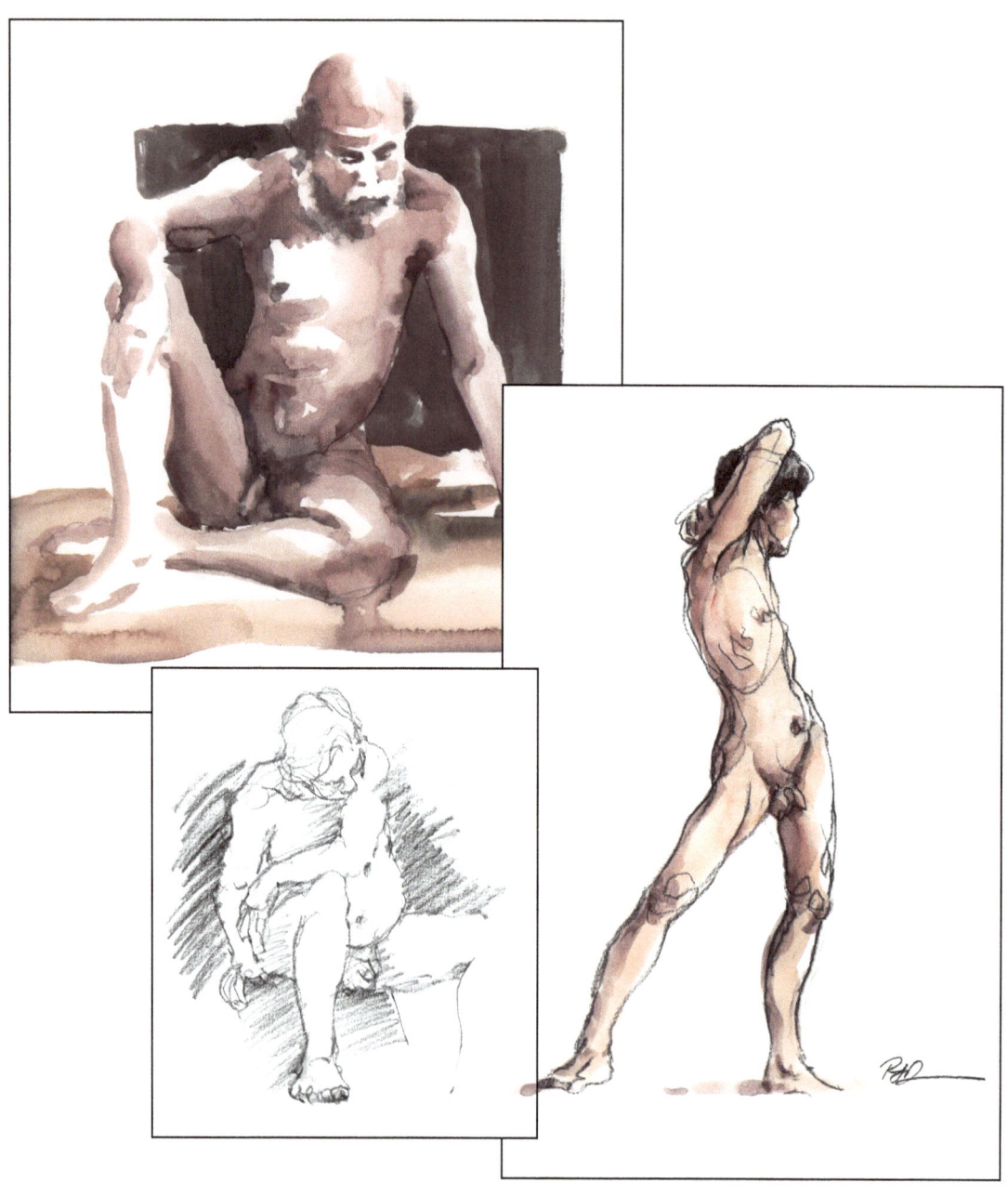

# *Let's start drawing...*

The purpose of this book is to help you paint convincing figures. Drawing leads to painting, and painting means, simply, that you are drawing in paint. Too many aspiring arists stumble when they finally pick up a paint brush. Admittedly, starting to paint is an emotional jump. However, whatever medium you use, there is little to stumble over if you remember that you are simply drawing with a medium instead of a pencil or pen.

**H**aving absorbed my short course on anatomy for artists, I feel confident that you have enough knowledge to apply what you have learned. Now, concentrate on putting figures into your paintings. Your biggest concern will be obtaining good models. Large cities usually offer a better selection of models simply because of the larger population. That said, welcome the discipline and the challenge every week.

I have found that in landscape painting, active figures add immense interest. Look around, at your next visit to a group art show, and notice how few paintings carry convincing figures. Many that do include figures are slavishly copied photographs. If the artist really knows how to use photographs as an aid, not as a crutch – no problem. Too often that is not the case.

From here on, your task is to train your eye, not your hand, not your pencil or pen. You will find that, slowly, your hand and your eye will grow closer together. It won't happen by tomorrow. It is not a short trip, and the universal question – Are we there yet?- will echo in your mind. And

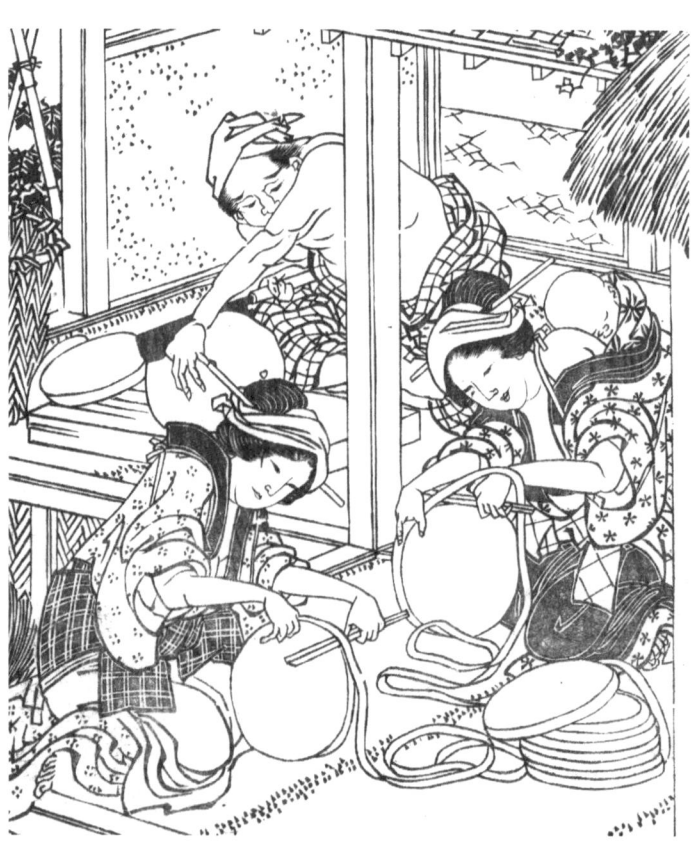

Hokusai Manga-Vol. 13. Private collection

"No" you are not there yet. Neither am I. And that is the paradox in this whole business of art. We strive to improve and we work our whole lives pursuing a chimera, an illusion that we will reach our goal. I am constantly reminded of the Japanese master Hokusai's death-bed exclaimation.

*"If only Heaven will give me just another ten years... Just another five more years, then I could become a real painter."*

Alas, I wish you the same lament. It is the mark of a true artist...always learning, always striving. It is also the mark of a life well lived.

# The One Minute Pose

The most frightening life class segment is the one-minute pose that starts many sessions. Remember, the purpose is two-fold: to help the artist to loosen up and to try to encompass the entirety of the figure, while capturing the flow of energy on display. The charge is to draw the whole figure in one or two minutes.

An instructor may guide you, but he or she will not, and should not, criticize your attempts. No one is looking to see verisimilitude. The class is too busy fighting the same bug-a-boos as are you.

First comes the time clock. You can make it your friend because, realistically, few can easily capture the dynamic of a good pose in one minute. So who can, or will, criticize your effort? Drawing is all about observation and observation is a learning process. Eventually the distance between your brain and your fingertips becomes shortened.

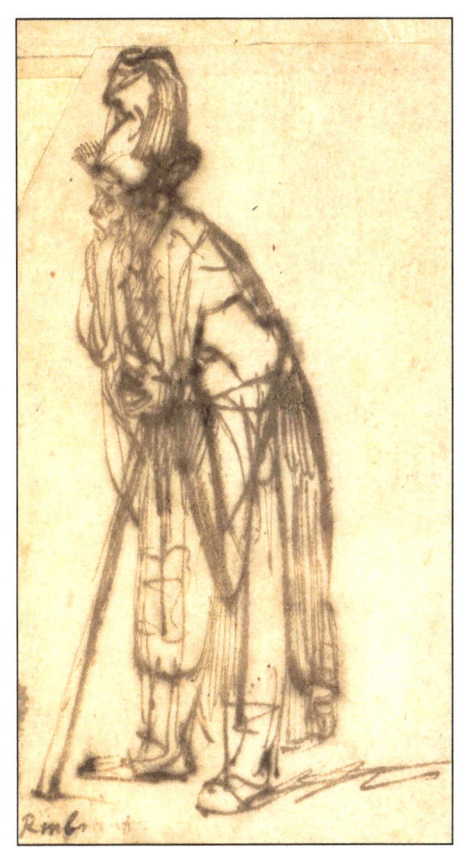

Rembrandt van Rijn
Old Man Leaning On a Stick, 1635-40
pen and brown ink 5 5/16 x 3 1/16
The Metropolitan Museum of Art,
Robert Lehman Collection.
1975.1.796

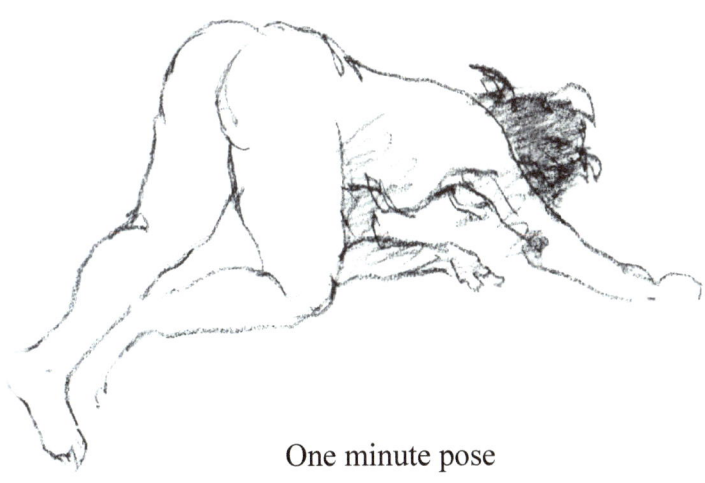

One minute pose

It is a complex interplay of mind-body dynamics. Don't be discouraged by your results. It takes practice, and I have been practicing a long time. Even though I go to life class every week, some weeks are productive and some produce little that is worthwhile.

A number of years ago I walked up the Grand Staircase at the Metropolitan Museum of Art, and at the top of the stairs I saw a small Rembrandt pen and brown ink drawing of an old man, leaning on a stick. It was all of 5" 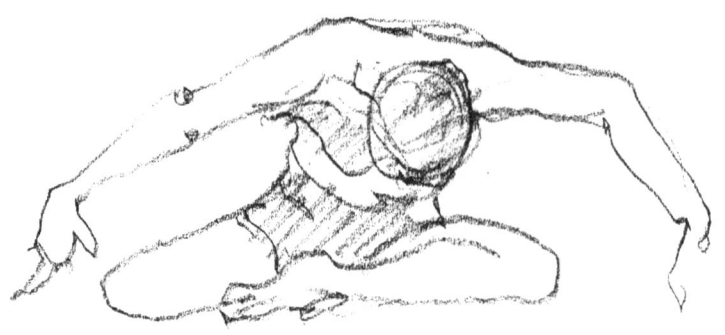 high and probably took a minute or two, at the most, for the master to produce. It made my entire trip to the Met worthwhile, and I hadn't yet seen the exhibit for which I came. Rembrandt was the master of the quick sketch and was also known to carry small copper plates of various sizes in his pocket, should the occasion arise that demanded a quick engraving.

## Seeing: There's The Rub

Few people realize that seeing is a mental process that involves a complex interplay of many areas of the brain. We have all been subject to the old high school biology book comparison sketch on how the eye sees. The eye has been likened to the camera ever since the camera was invented. A common textbook diagram compared the camera's lens and film to the lens and retina in the eye. Since Johannes Kepler (1571-1630), we knew an image was recorded upside down, but the new-born brain rather quickly recognized that, and reversed it. Then medical science slowly began to discover that those nerve impulses were not simply recorded, as a photo to be read, but rather needed to be interpreted for us to understand what we were seeing. Today we can count over 30 regions that take part in our ability to "see." [9]

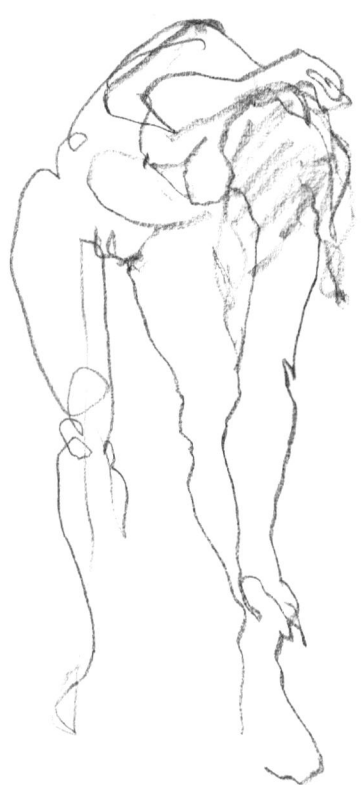

One minute poses

9. Noback's Human Nervous System. Humana Press New York 7th Edition, 2005. p.334.

Sight is not the simple process of recording a scene but rather the beginning of the process of interpreting it so we can function in our complex world. Evidence of this is becoming more apparent every day. Eye witness testimony, a mainstay of criminal investigations for centuries, has fallen from favor under the weight of a great many instances of faulty memory. We see what we want to see, see what we know, and see what we have learned. Sight is so much more than a physical phenomenon.

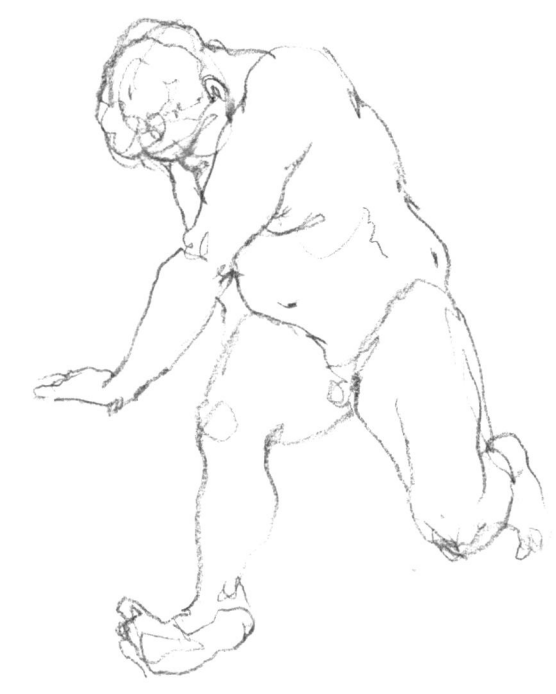

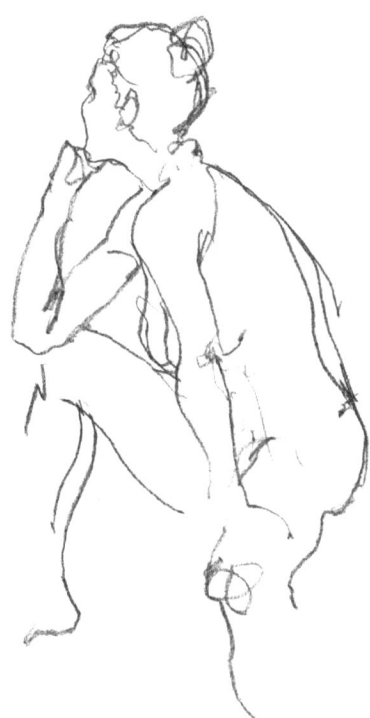

Three one minute poses

For those who are discouraged by their skill level in drawing the figure, know that like so much in life, it takes work. Or, as Ralph Waldo Emerson said, ***"Do the thing and you will have the power."*** That's an enduring reminder that it is a learning process. And that your ability will grow as you work at the task.

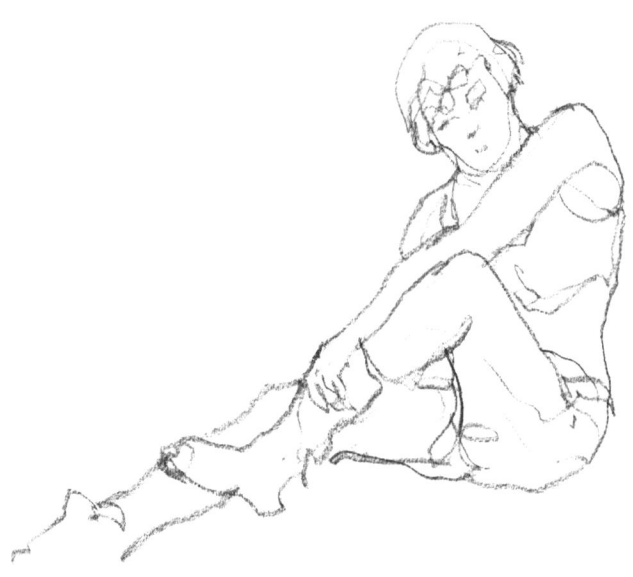

# Gesture Drawing

The very thought that you are "drawing" the figure works against you in life class. We think of drawing as an exercise aimed at capturing the subject on paper. Instead, how about thinking of capturing the action on paper and leaving drawing a likeness to another day when time is independent? Nicolaides emphasizes feeling the action in your own body. This helps you get away from all the prejudices that the act of drawing has instilled in your mind.

Eventually, gesture drawing will become an integral part of all of your drawing. A good example of gesture drawing's power is the courtroom artist. They have to capture the personality of a defendant or a prosecutor by his or her stance, face, arm movement, and do it quickly. The litigants are not in court to pose for sketches. The flick of a wrist or the importance of a frown can be the linchpin in capturing the personality of a prosecutor or the impotence of the accused. The gesture need not be exaggerated physical action. As you get more experienced (more observant) you will note smaller actions carrying enormous impact. Slumping shoulders, a wan smile, or a feeble arm movement often show everything you want to say.

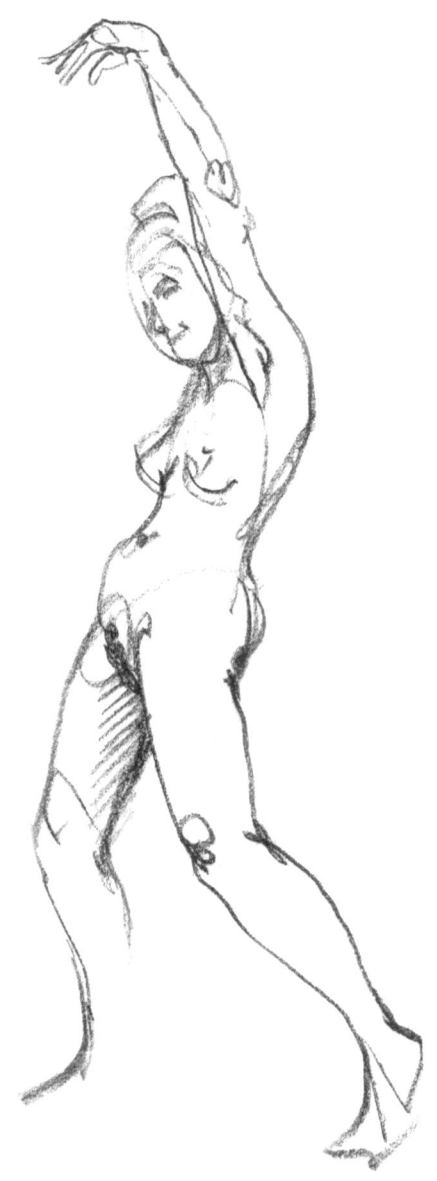

One minute is enough time to capture an exuberant pose.

In every life class you will see beginners struggling to "build" a figure. You see them measuring the figure with their pencil or checking to see how many heads make up the height of figure. This breaks that invisible bond stretchng from your hand to your model. Drawing is an "all in" proposition. That's why gesture drawing is more than a method; it is inculcation, an immersion, into an approach that takes over your whole artistic being. You draw, you feel, there is no separation.

Too often our sight is inadequate for the task. Of course, for the artist who wants to record and interpret a scene, shortening the distance between his brain and fingertips is more than just a fancy phrase. It is a complex interplay of mind-body dynamics. And I must repeat it again – there is no shortcut in this pursuit.

It is worthwhile to bear in mind what Rodin did. He *"..drew from the model while hardly glancing at his pencil so as to free his hand for inventing more boldly than it would dare under the constant censure of his eye."* [10]

And no one would say that Rodin wasn't a realist.

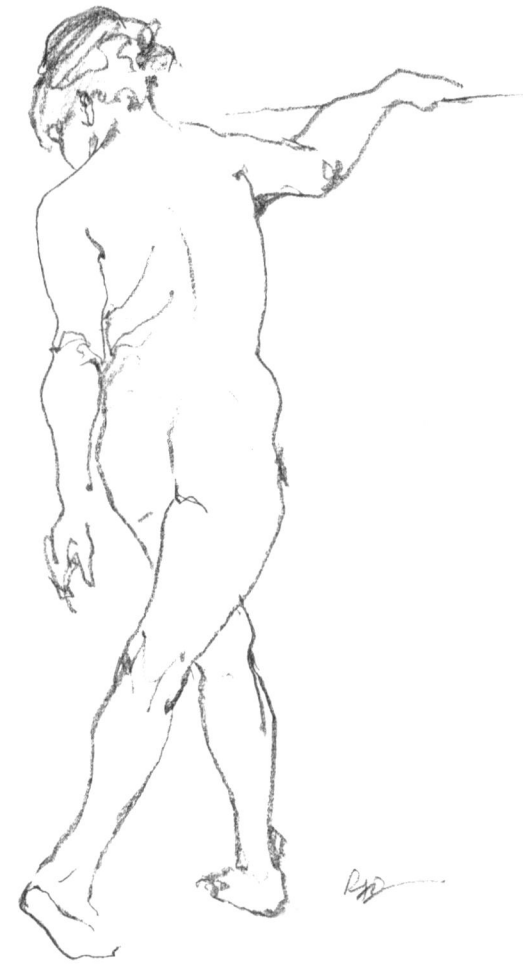

I think he was pursuing the essence of the model – attempting to capture the energy inherent in every pose. It is interesting to recall that when he was sculpting his powerful figures, many people accused him of making casts of real people. From our place and in our time, it is hard to believe that accusation. However, such was the emotional power of his work that their belief was understandable.

I believe that the Nicolaides method is the best approach to eventual mastery of the kind of figure that you want to end up on your sketchpad, canvas, or watercolor paper. Not only will you gain control of the allotted paper space but also begin to grasp the entirety of the figure in your mind's eye. This is good to keep in mind when you start quick poses.

10. A. Hyatt Mayor. Artists & Anatomists. The Metropolitan Museum of Art 1984

Monet used to tell his models, "talk, laugh, move.... to look real you must be alive." Capturing that movement is the biggest challenge you will face. Once again, go to any local art show, look for the figure paintings, and ask yourself how many of the figures look alive. You will come back to life class with a renewed dedication and a clearer idea of what you are after.

Spread over this page are three figures, done at different times, with different models. All are one or two minutes poses, each trying to capture the spontaniety expressed by the model. You can see some contour drawing showing up in various degrees as I sketched, without worrying about anything except capturing a feeling. Go for liveliness, not verisimilitude.

# Gesture Drawings in Ink and Steel

The accompanying photo of a commissioned, steel Predator Hawk© sculpture shows how Wendy Klemperer captures the predatory action of a hawk early in the production process. Wendy says, "I often describe the process of my work as three-dimensional gesture drawing." That's gesture drawing in steel! But once you see how she starts her sculpture, it all makes sense. And once her client saw this stage of her work, capturing the essence of predation, it was full speed ahead!

Gesture is energy and energy is life. Whether you draw people or animals, sketch birds or zebras, it is more than the static copy of nature that you are after. It is an attitude, a look, a posture, and an insight into a creature's very being. Impossible to capture? Just note how quickly you can identify a friend or a neighbor from behind, or at a distance. We are all individuals. That individuality is what we are after in our art, and it only comes when we're comfortable with our tools and clear about our goal.

Predator Hawk (client approval stage) by Wendy Klemperer

Bill Logan has been painting his cats for a long time. He now has over 500 cat drawings in his file. He knows them so well that he has even sketched some of them with his eyes closed! Most of them capture the essence of "cat." It is not too big a jump from Bill's pursuit to yours. Capturing the essence of a living creature, be it a cat, a mouse or a fellow human being presents the same challenge. If you have a pet, you have a live model with you at home! Take advantage of it.

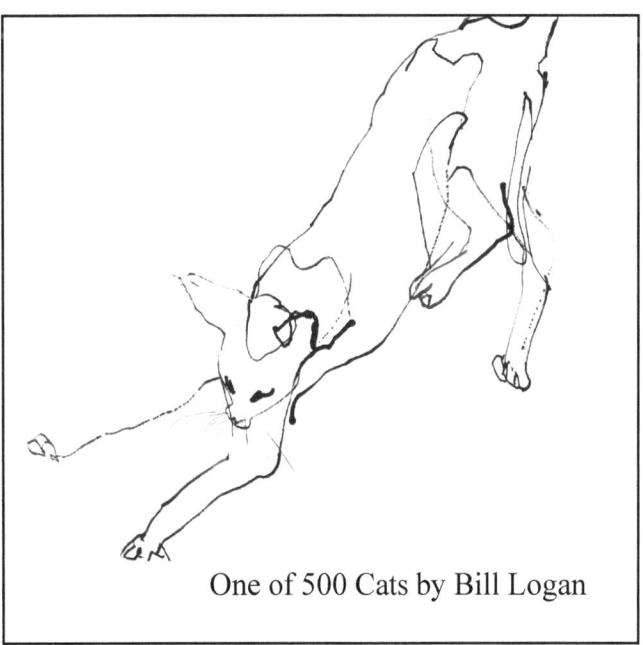

One of 500 Cats by Bill Logan

**Egon Schiele (1890-1918).** His mother said Egon drew pictures from the age of two. Whether he really started that early or not, there is no denying his talent. He is mostly known for his superb figurative work. His dramatic, erotic, and powerful art, while not appealing to everyone, should be an inspiration to any aspiring artist. He died, at the age of 28, a few days after his wife, in the Spanish Influenza epidemic of 1918. As with Van Gogh, we lost a superb artist much too early.

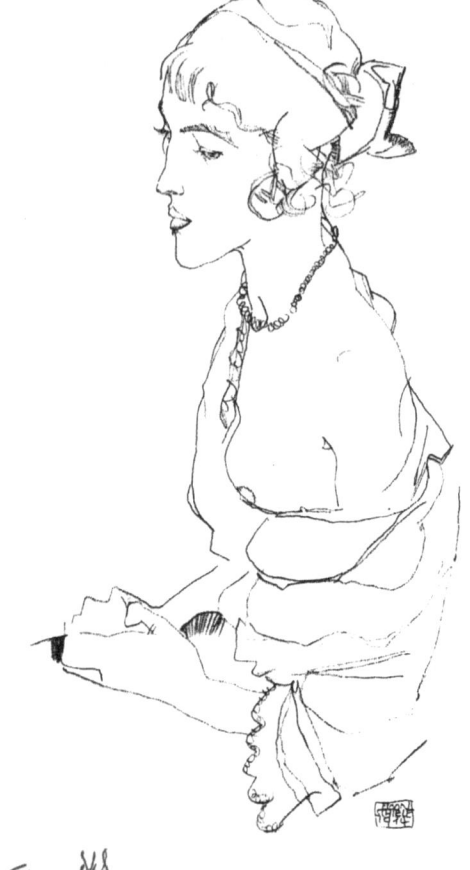

Poldi by Egon Schiele (1890-1918)

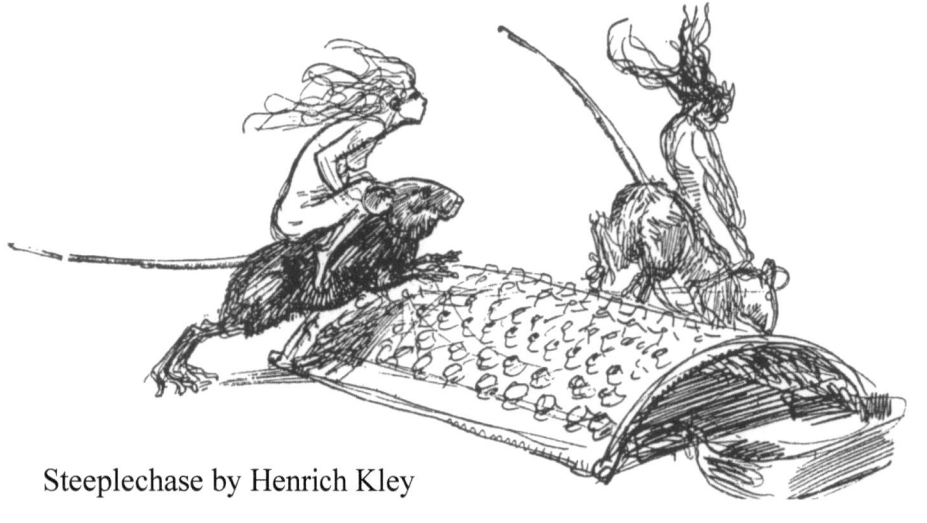

Steeplechase by Henrich Kley

**Heinrich Kley.** He was born in Germany, in the area known as the Rhineland in 1863, and died sometime in the 1940's. He is well known for his cartoons and social satire, enhanced by his brilliant, facile linework. I chose to reproduce the food grater jumping rats, but he sketched every kind of animal, many in human-like activities for his satirical work. Everything he produced exhibited energy and aliveness.

70

# Moving from Gesture to Contour Drawing

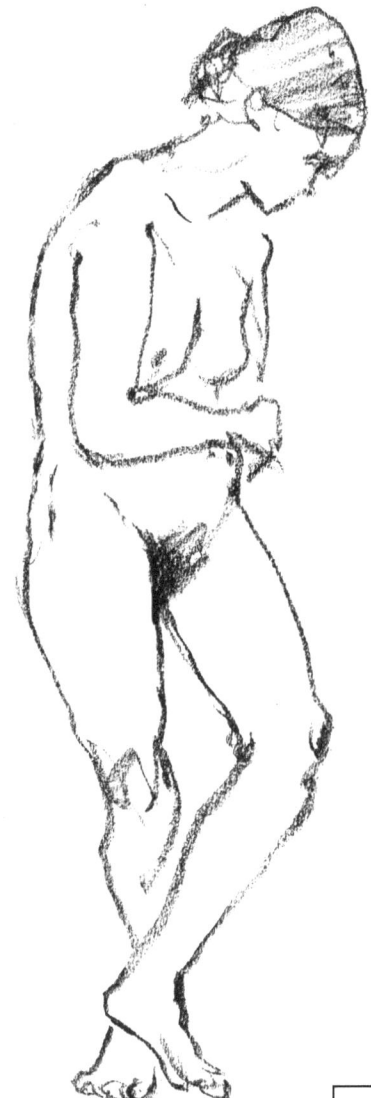

**E**ventually, your gesture drawings will meld with your contour drawings and you will not think about these two separate approaches to drawing. You will just "draw." The secret is to keep the liveliness in your drawings of the figures all the way to your canvas or watercolor paper.

Not only will this approach help you gain control of the paper space but you will also begin to grasp the entire figure in your mind's eye. Eventually, gesture drawing will become an integral part of all of your drawing. Your gesture work should not be reserved for exaggerated physical action. As you get more experienced (more observant) you will note smaller actions carrying enormous impact. Slumping shoulders, a wan smile, or a feeble arm movement often show everything you want to say. Don't worry about wrong marks. No need to erase a wayward line. Let your struggle and your thinking show.

**Short poses showing gesture and contour drawings begin to merge.**

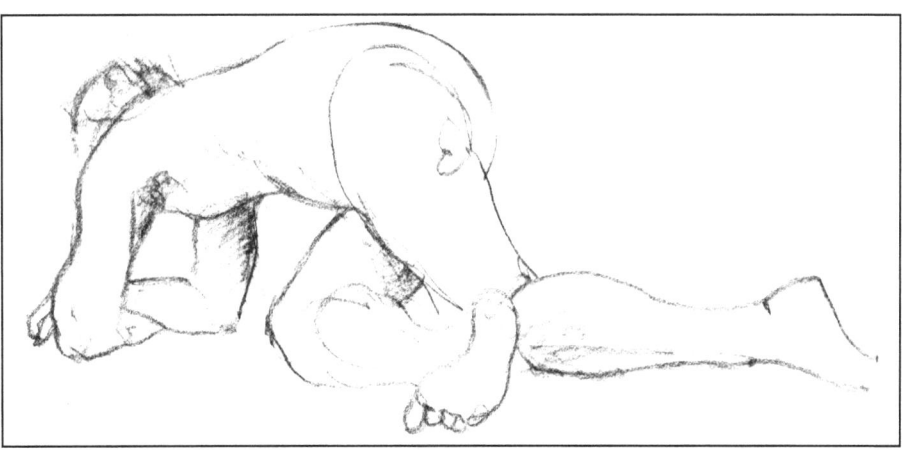

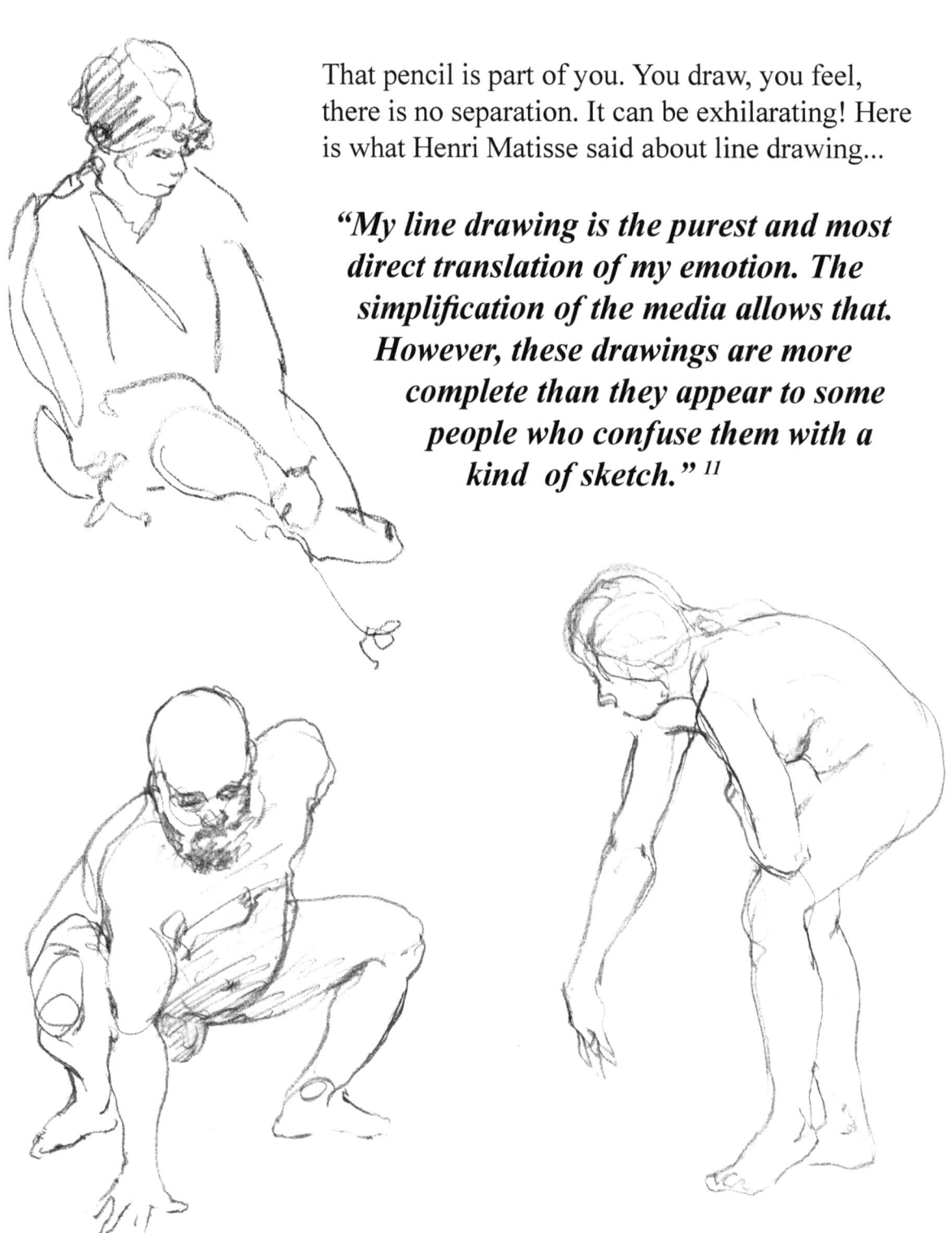

That pencil is part of you. You draw, you feel, there is no separation. It can be exhilarating! Here is what Henri Matisse said about line drawing...

*"My line drawing is the purest and most direct translation of my emotion. The simplification of the media allows that. However, these drawings are more complete than they appear to some people who confuse them with a kind of sketch."* [11]

11. Matisse on Art. Jack Flam University of California Press, 1995 P. 130

Because there are no lines on the figure, it allows the artist to capture the figure with freedom. Because strict adherence to the "rules" no longer pertains.

### Nicolaides says, "You should draw, not what the thing looks like, not even what it is, but what it is doing."

This is good to keep in mind when you start quick poses. Go after the aliveness and don't worry about figure proportions. This will help you gain control of the allotted paper space and also you will begin to grasp the entirety of the figure in your minds eye.

Sometimes, after a gesture session I find that nothing I have produced is worth a second look. You, too, will have times when you feel discouraged. Remember, it is difficult to assess one's progress up close. Only with the distance time affords will your progress show itself.

I like what Andrew Wyeth says. "I'll take weeks doing drawings and watercolor studies that I may never use... I feel that the communion that has seeped into my subconscious will eventually come out in the final picture."[12] I believe that this is his way of saying that progress is not something you can measure day to day. Experience just piles up in a untidy way and one day it sorts itself out and looks back at you from your work with a smile. You just have to stay on the path and keep the faith.

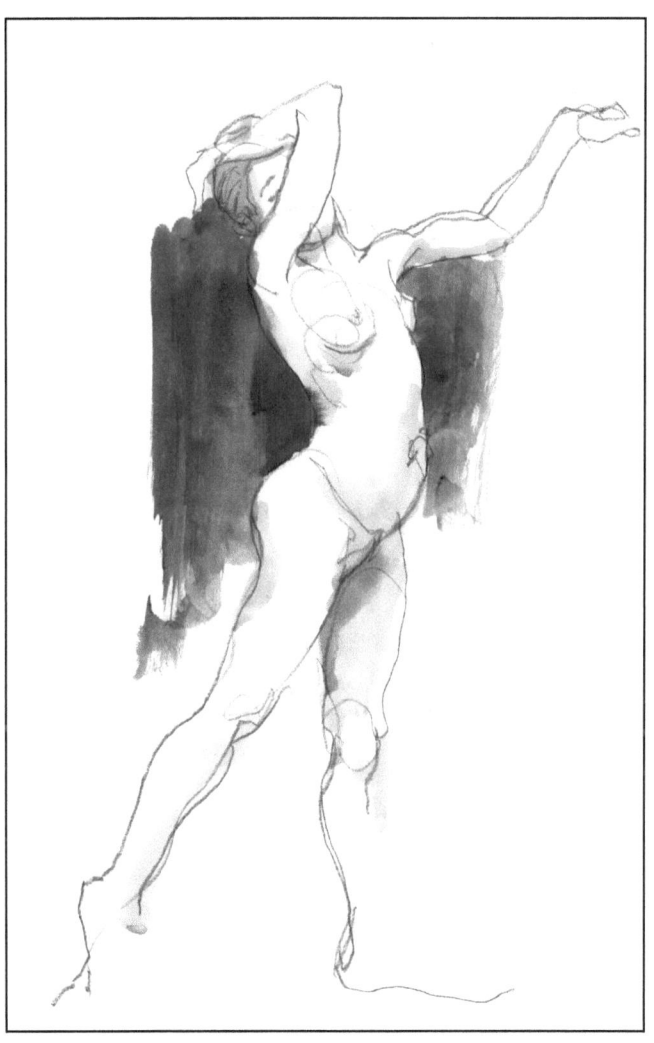

A little background to offset the figure adds interest to a quick 5 minute sketch.

12. The Art of Andrew Wyeth. Wanda Corn The Fine Arts Museums of San Francisco, California 1973. p 70

# Contour Drawing

Contour drawing seems like the polar opposite of gesture drawing and in many ways it is. With gesture drawing you are chasing the action, trying to harness the energy in the pose. With contour drawing you are looking for the edges that define the figure. We see and relate to edges. With contour drawing you want your pencil or pen to closely follow the body contours of the model. It is as if the point of your pen or pencil is on the body and slowly traveling over every bulge and depression as it describes the figure. This exercise sharpens your ability to observe the differences in every pose and the uniqueness in every person. Some advocates of contour drawing insist that you do not look at the paper while drawing. I find this restriction almost impossible to adhere to. The temptation to reposition your pencil cannot, and need not, be ignored. The discipline needed to marry your pencil's movement to the distance your eyes travel is of paramount importance. They must move in concert. Eventually the two featured approaches to drawing the model – gesture and contour - will meld into one and you will simply be "drawing." This will be an entirely unconscious evolution as your comfort level and experience blends these two methods together. By capturing the action with gesture drawing and combining it with the exacting contours of the body, a certain artistic truth will emerge.

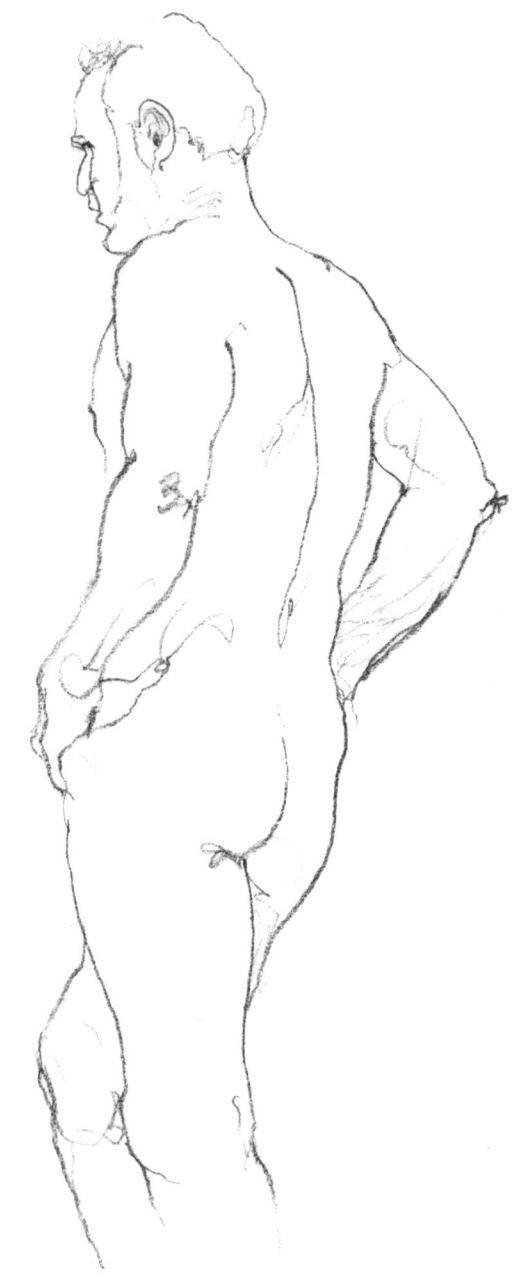

You want to feel that you are in physical contact with the model and that your pencil and your eyes are moving as one. This is a blending that is devoutly to be wished and should be ardently pursued by every artist working in the realist mode.

Don't try to hurry this melding of gesture and contour. Don't even think about it. Stay a student while in class. Think of this as a ball player thinks of batting practice; something the pros never eliminate in their careers. Once you step out of class, it is then that you are not a student. What you are doing in class is trying to improve by training your eyes to see.

Considering the fact that artists, like all sighted people, have used their eyes since they were born, it is very hard to convince people that seeing is a learning experience. We really see with our brain. What we call seeing is a construct of many different images. Scientists, using scanning devices have recorded the way our eye captures a scene.

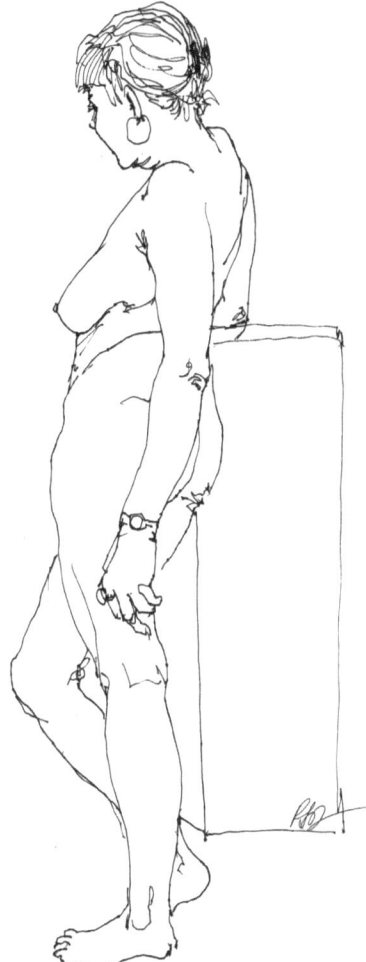

Each movement, called a saccade, lasts just a fraction of a second, a millisecond, as we build a construct with our brain and that enables us to "see." It makes sense that the more observant we are, the more invested in the subject, the more we will really see.

Just think of how much more you see and understand while visiting a museum exhibition, particularly when you accompany a docent or a curator on a tour. Or, the excitement you felt the first time you walked in the woods with a naturalist.

With contour drawing you want your line to say as much as possible about the figure you are describing with your pencil or pen. That means that you are chasing much more than an outline or silhouette. Obviously there are no outlines on the figure.

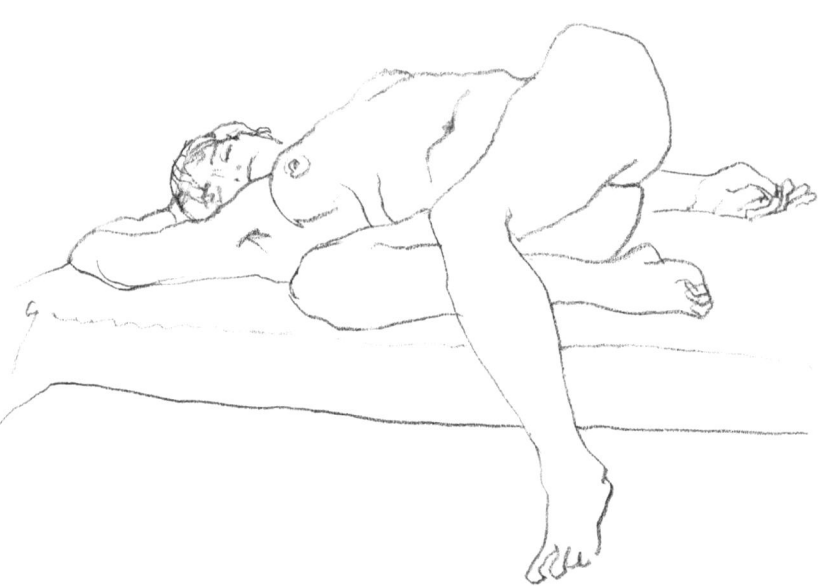

When a muscle's bulge makes its presence known to your pencil, your drawing takes a step forward. Every change in your line is evidence of your increased observation skills.

## Push–pull

The line you use can vary – should vary. By that, I mean you can push it into the paper and pull it toward you depending upon the depth of various aspects of the model's body. Feel it. The line might not look like it is varying very much but it will change, and you will be feeling the structure as you draw. That feeling is the secret behind drawing – good drawing.

## Drawing with a ruler?

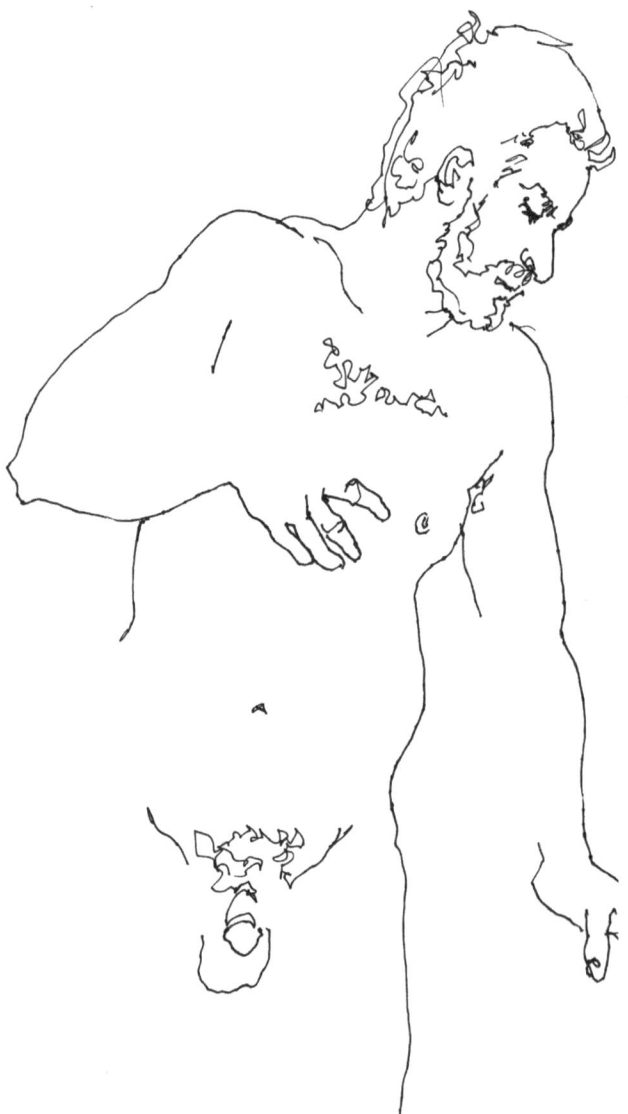

You really cannot draw a lively figure with a ruler. O.K., no one would try to do that. However, some books would have you using building blocks, squares, and triangles to construct a figure, section by section. I've seen the head divided into

76

rectangles and squares. Some books divide every part of the body into head sizes. They show the legs as 4 heads long. The male is shown as 7 1/2 heads tall and, often, so is the female.

You could easily find people who would fit these measurements but few bodies follow these balanced proportions and exact measurements. Many of the statues by famous Greek sculptors, such as Polykleitos, were intended to present an ideal. However, we are here to draw real people, different people, from different perspectives, and no ruler, or exact measurements will aid you in doing that.

No less an artist than Leonardo da Vinci (1452-1519) addressed this very subject a long time ago.

*"...a man can still be in proportion and be fat or tall and thin or medium and whoever does not take account of such variety, will cast his figures in one mould so that they will all appear to be brothers and this practice deserves great censure."* [13]

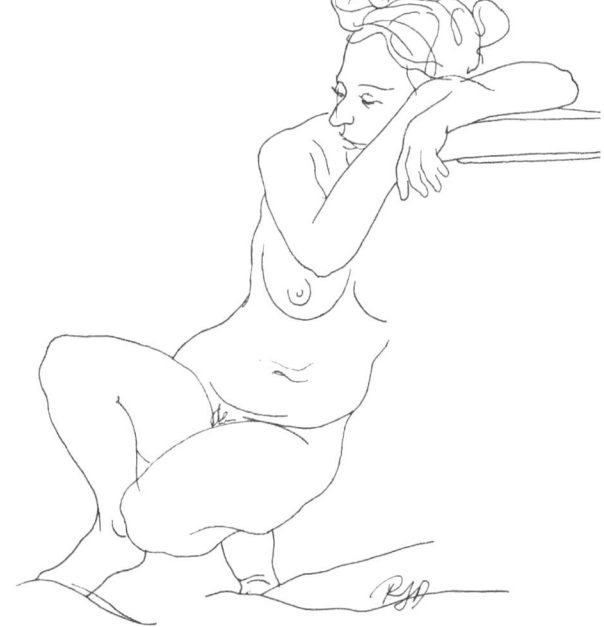

So, go to your model to further your understanding of how to draw the figure.

13. Leonardo on Painting  Edit by Martin Kemp. Yale University Press, New Haven. 1989. p.199

# Only One Way to Draw the Figure ?

**J**ust because I advocate gesture drawing as the gateway approach to drawing the figure doesn't mean that my line drawing approach to gesture, evidenced by examples of my work, is the only way to produce a quick sketch. Your particular style is embedded in your training, your personality, and your experiences in life. For that reason and to make my point, I chose two quick sketches, done by a fellow artist with whom I share weekly life class sessions.

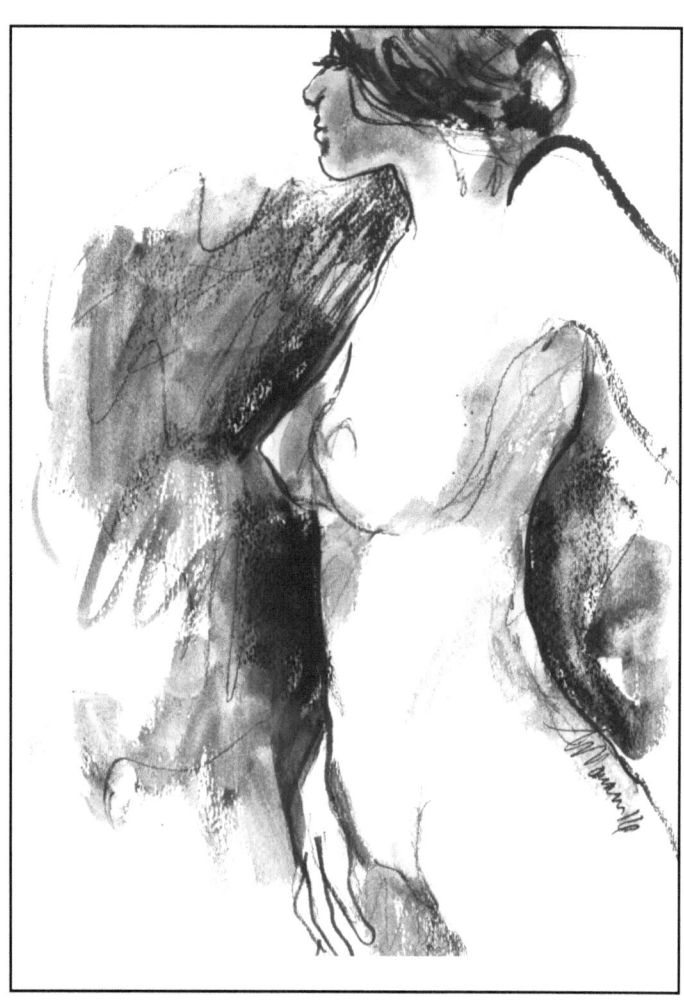

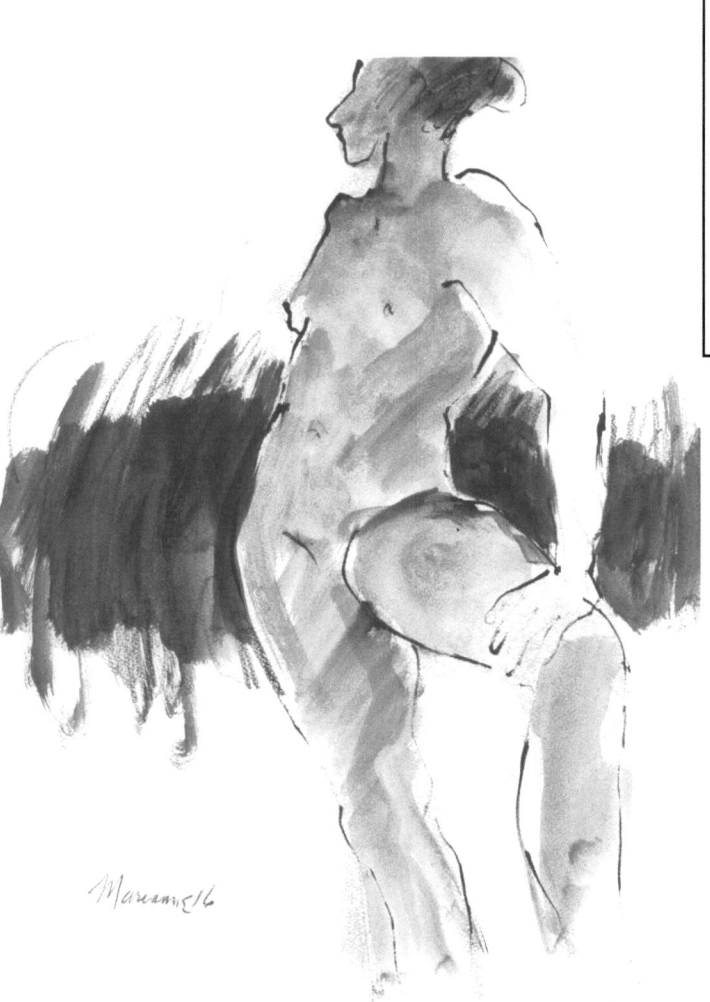

Any one of these sketches can stand alone, complete, and exemplary. Every artist looking at the same pose, will treat it differently. That is to be expected and encouraged. Consider these two inspiring examples by Marianne VanBlarcom.

# Longer Drawing Sessions

The one, two, and five minute poses make up my favorite part of a life class. Some call it warm up time, but it really is an opportunity to get control of the figure as it relates to the sheet or pad of paper on which you are working. Paper is cheap, don't skimp by working too small, as it cramps your ability to get your whole arm into the act of drawing. It is in these short sessions that control becomes part of your competence. The short poses are quickly over and soon you are drawing longer poses - just don't tighten up.

# Longer Drawing Sessions

## The 5 Minute Pose

What a luxury!  Now you have five full minutes to draw the figure. No "clock police" to blow the whistle, and an opportunity to really grab the figure and wrestle it onto the paper. You may even have time to add a little color or black & white wash. I must caution you not to slip back into a cramped stroke and lose the freedom you have gained by your more energetic approach to the figure through the gesture drawing. Remember to draw with your whole arm, not just with the tips of your tense fingers.

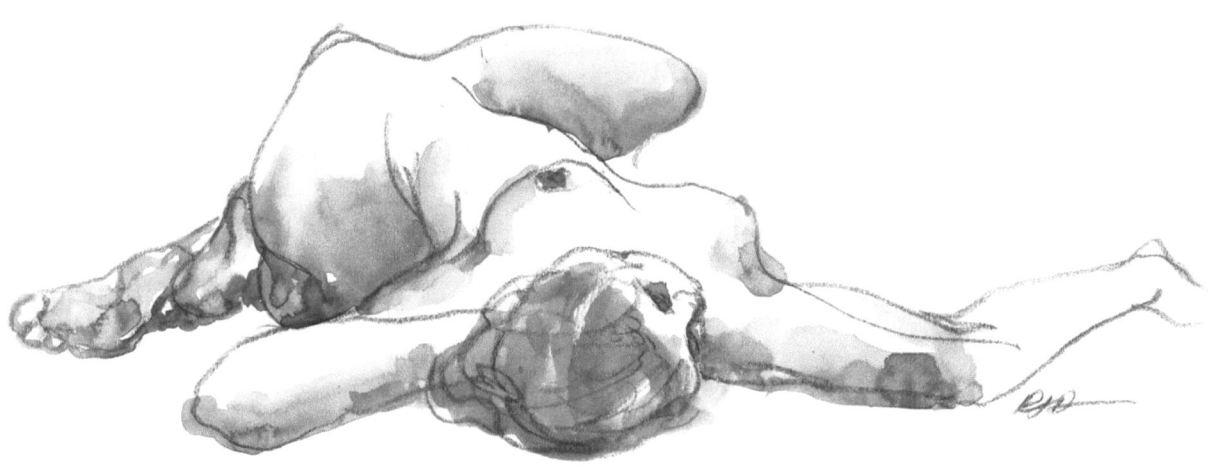

Five minute pose in line and black wash.

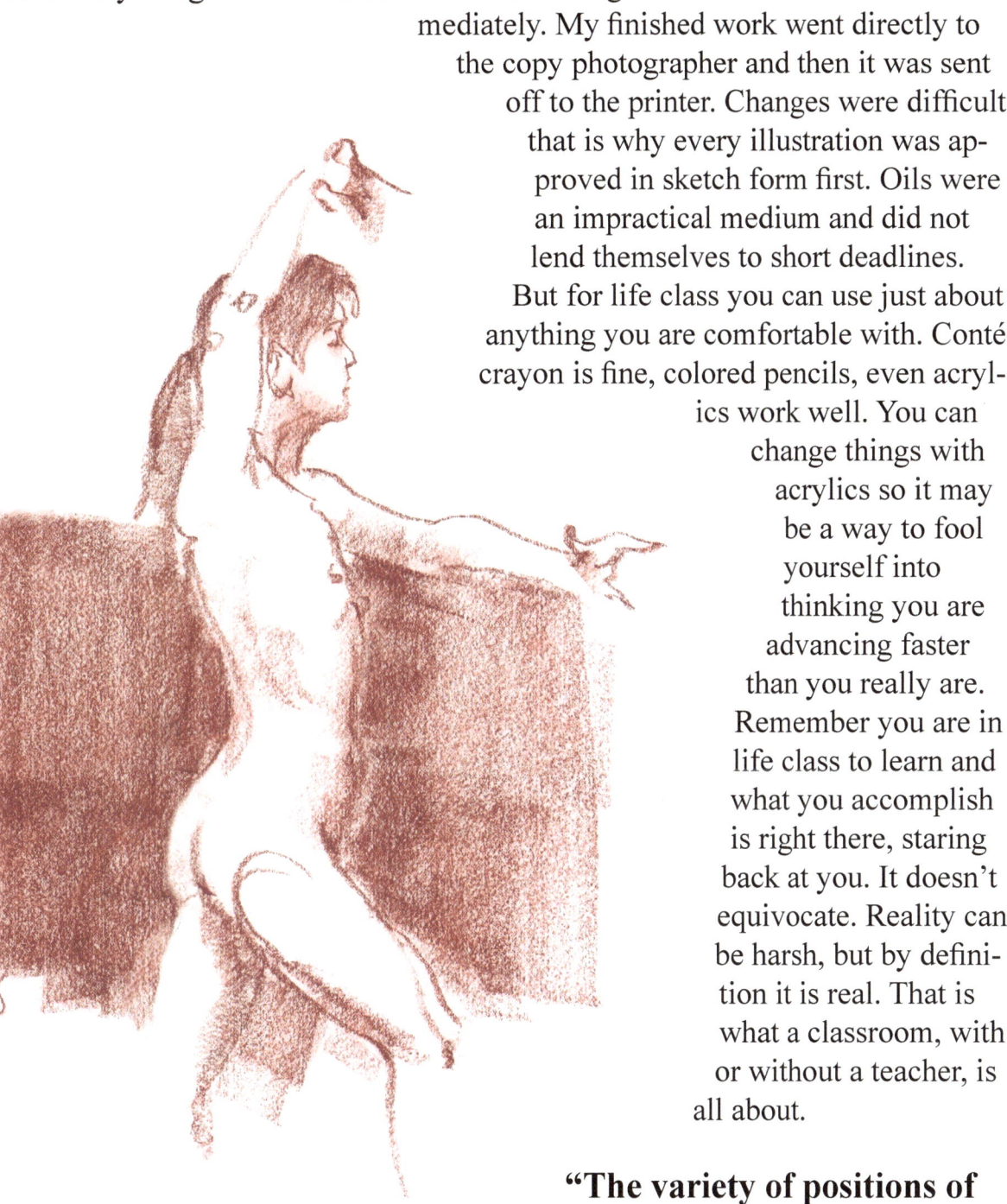

**W**atercolor may not be your medium. That's okay. I have a love hate relationship with it myself. I used it professionally in my medical work because I was busy from sun up to sun down turning out work for medical journals and texts and every thing was on a deadline. The advantage was that watercolor dried immediately. My finished work went directly to the copy photographer and then it was sent off to the printer. Changes were difficult, that is why every illustration was approved in sketch form first. Oils were an impractical medium and did not lend themselves to short deadlines. But for life class you can use just about anything you are comfortable with. Conté crayon is fine, colored pencils, even acrylics work well. You can change things with acrylics so it may be a way to fool yourself into thinking you are advancing faster than you really are. Remember you are in life class to learn and what you accomplish is right there, staring back at you. It doesn't equivocate. Reality can be harsh, but by definition it is real. That is what a classroom, with or without a teacher, is all about.

**"The variety of positions of the shoulder is infinite."**[14]

14. Leonardo on Paintng. Edited by Marin Kemp. Yale UniversityPress.  p 137

## The Five Minute Pose
### - in line and watercolor

These sketches represent about as much effort as most models can exert in holding a pose for 5 minutes. They can stretch, bend or twist just enough in that time to make for an interesting session. By using your quick drawing skills you may even have time to throw in a bit of watercolor wash. It enlivens your sketch and is a good step in anyone's quest for mastery of watercolor. Again, no one expects a masteriece in 5 minutes, so have fun!

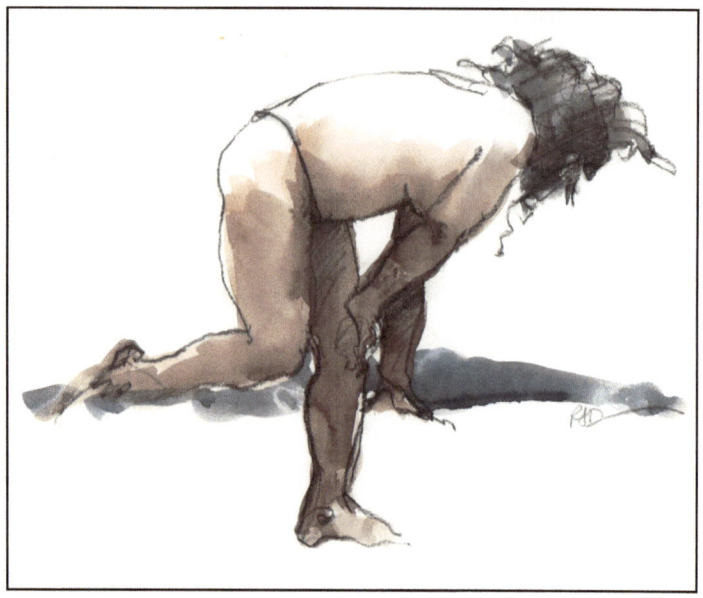

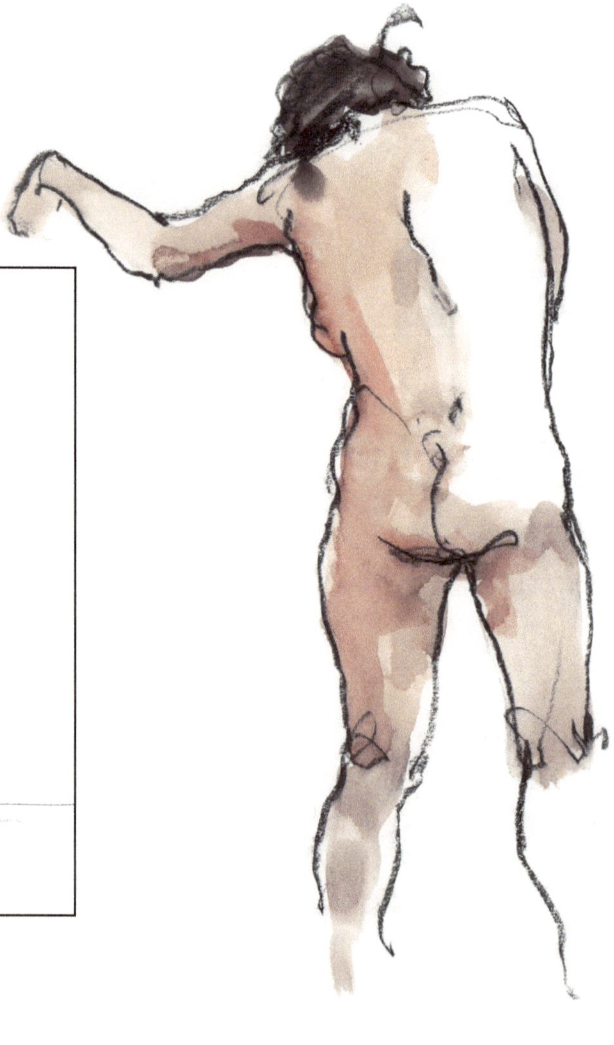

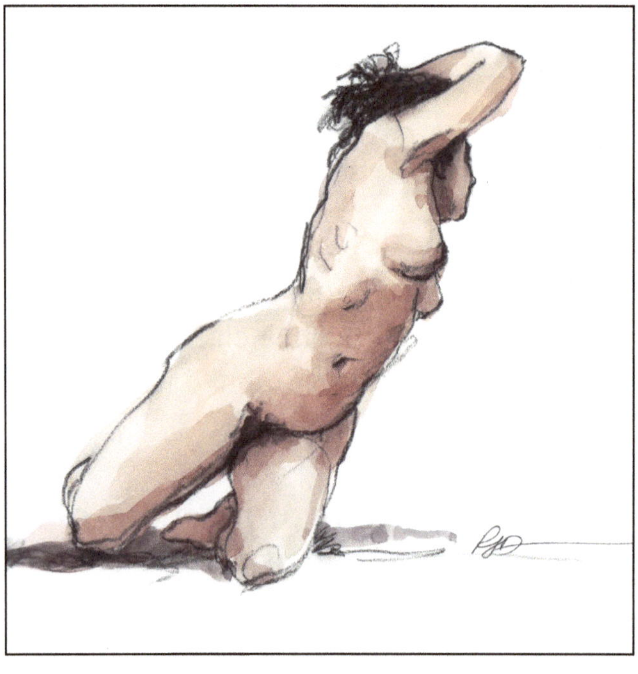

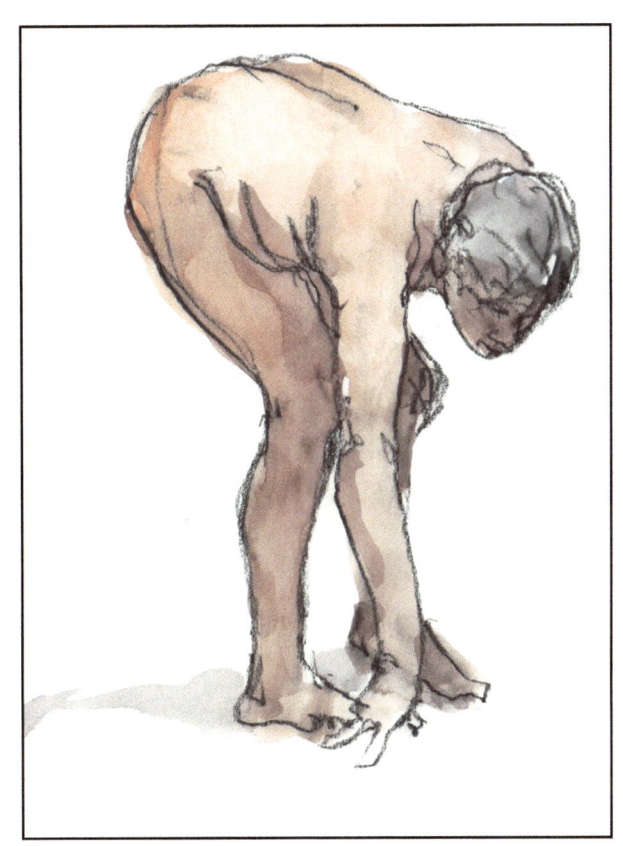

Here, once again, I selected a
few random 5 minute poses
that were done in charcoal pencil
and watercolor. There is just enough
bending and twisting to add interest
and it's still easy enough for the
model to hold the pose for that
time span.

# The Longer Pose – 20 Minutes to an Hour

The goal of all the foregoing exercises and study has been for you to arrive at the longer pose, one on which you can spend a little more time and not worry about the time clock. Different art classes will end with 20 minute poses, some end with an hour pose, and some painting classes can extend through several days. I think you can appreciate the dilemma. As the poses get longer, energy and liveliness is increasingly bled out. Of necessity, the pose becomes more sedentary. How is it possible for the model to keep that energy as he or she sits for a long pose, one you may even want to show as a finished painting? Think of the great painters of the past. Franz Hals managed to capture the personality of his sitters like few other artists.  Was it his enthusiasm for his work that was caught and picked up by the sitter? He often painted *alla prima,* boldly searching for that undefinable spark that lit up the sitter's face. I would argue that one or more of his sketches led to his decisions on a final pose that ultimately engaged the sitter's personality. Too many portrait artists rely too much on the camera. The camera can be an important tool in portraiture but remember that a photo shows an image of that person caught in a fraction of a second on a particular day, often under self conscious conditions. It is seldom the sum of a personality. If you are going to paint someone, you must get to know them, know their moods, their wants, their likes and dislikes. A portrait commission is not to be taken lightly. John Singer Sargent lamented his commissions for that very reason. However, he knew flattering portraits were related to his financial security. Portraiture was an important

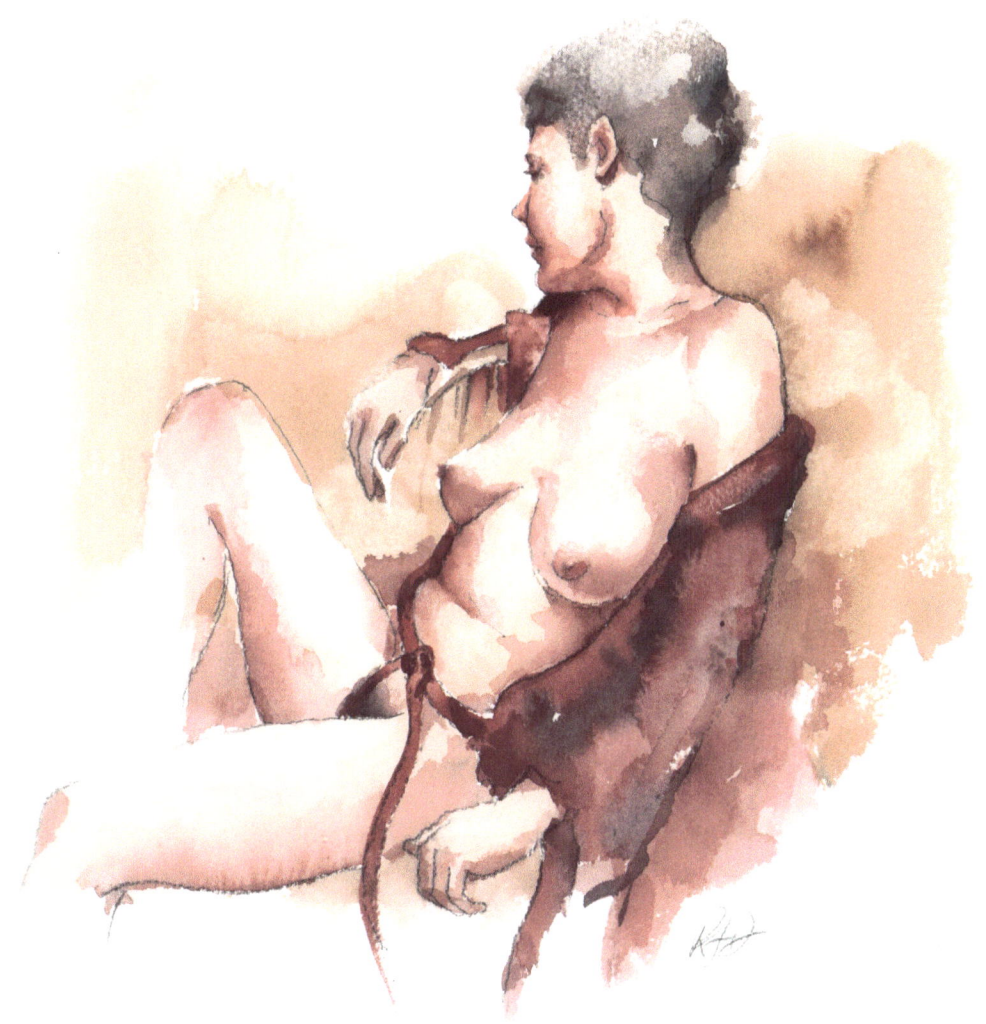

income source for Sargent but reportably it did not represent his favorite painting venue. Wealthy people do not relish paying healthy sums for unflattering portraits and Sargent knew that. His bravura brush stroked, handsome paintings, are often not representative of his best work, and only occasionally do they rise to great heights. Contrast that with Eakins. His portraits were so invasive, so brutal in their honesty, that few clients wanted to see themselves laid bare in that way. His portrait of his wife in a blue dress with her dog (Portrait of a Lady with a Setter Dog -1885)   shows so much about their relationship, about her feelings, that it hurts to look at it. Somewhere in between these two extremes there is a happy compromise, where the best aspects of a subject and his or her personality meet your best effort as an artist. With the exception of an occasional commisioned sporting painting, I try to avoid portraits.

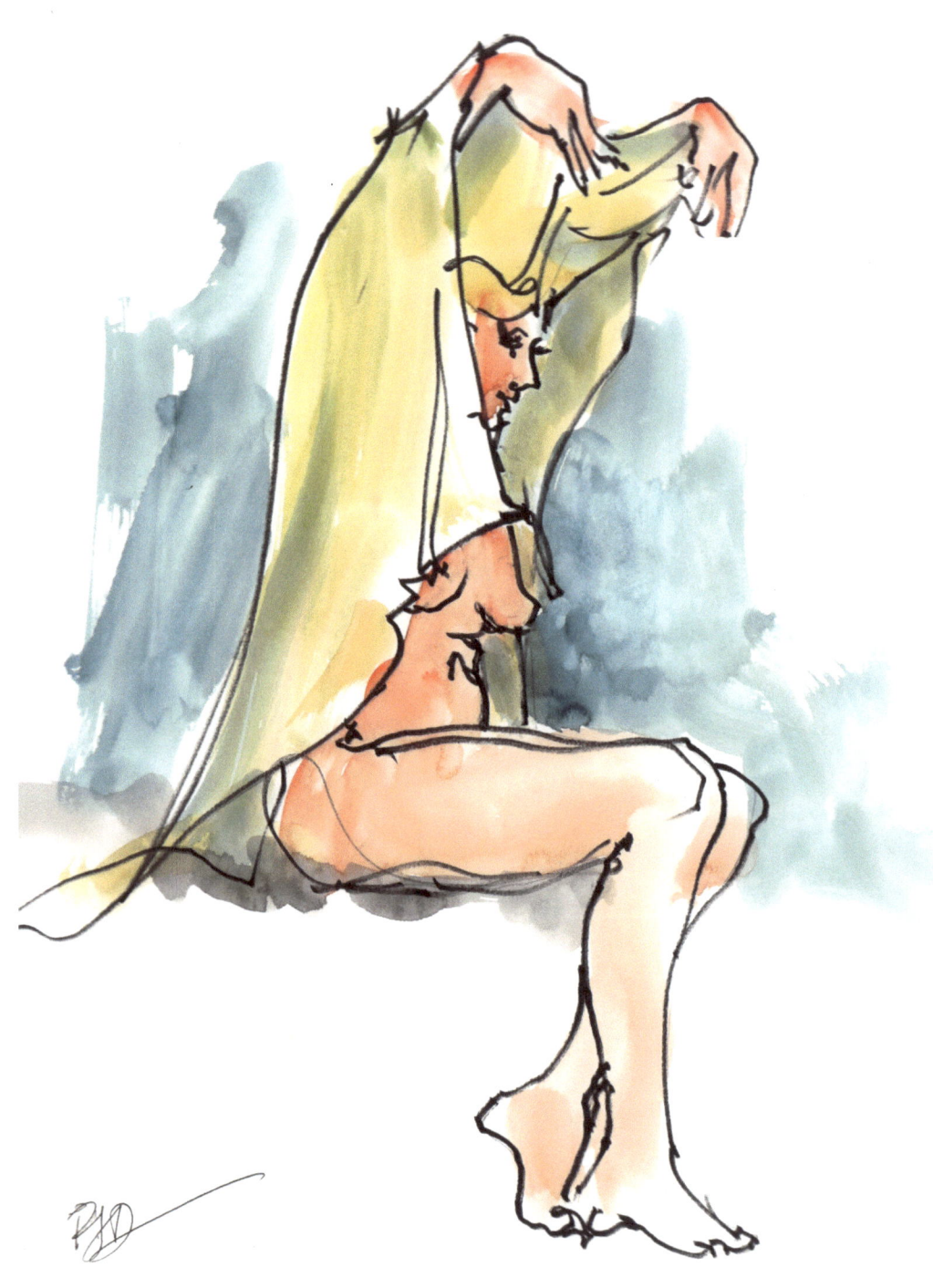

When you are feeling confident and like the pose, pick up a fine point, waterproof marker, and have at it. When you are done with your sketch, add some watercolor. Oft-times, you will catch the joy!

86

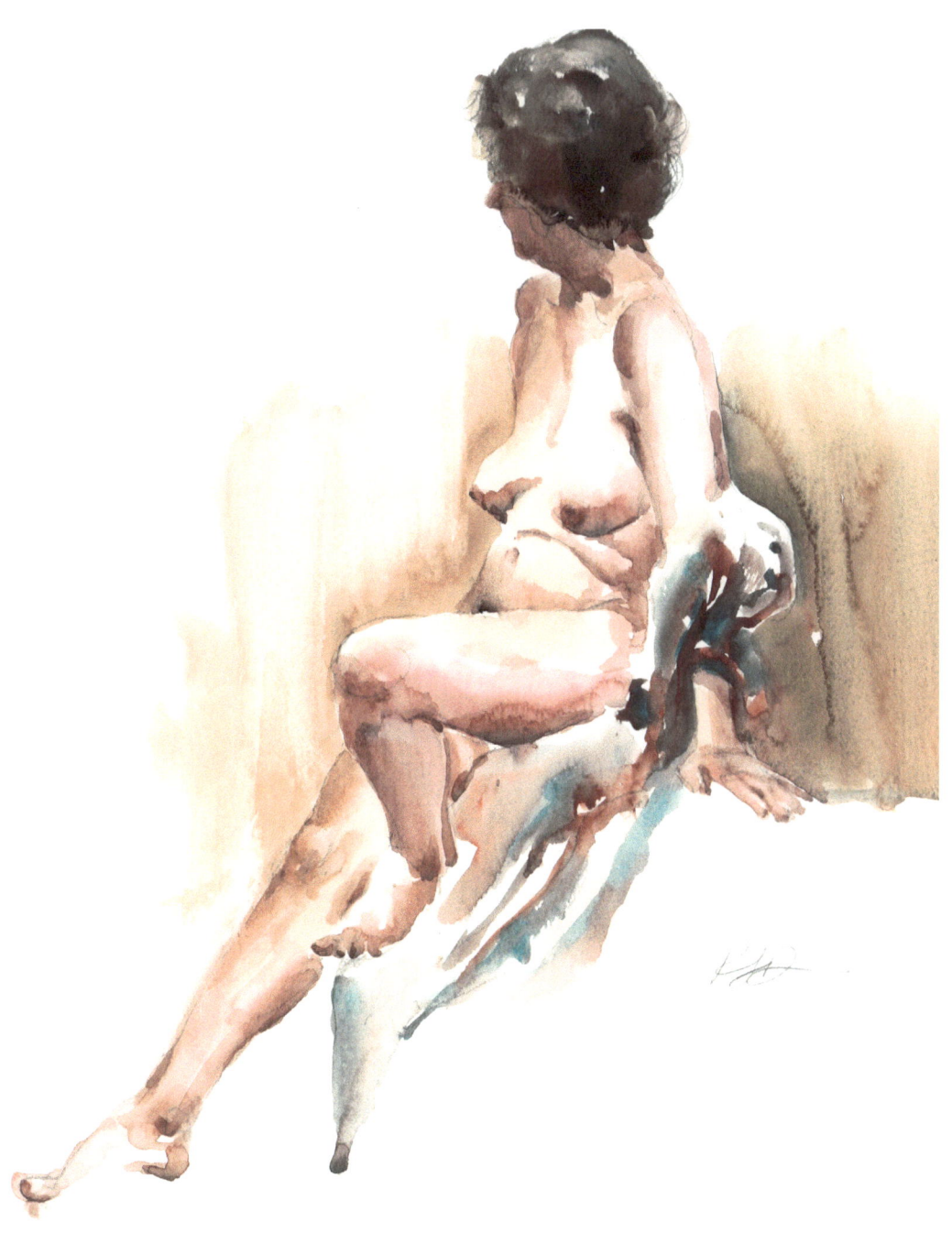

This sketch is the result of a one-hour pose, composed of two sessions with a rest break in between. Of necessity, the longer poses are more sedentary. The secret is to capture some of the personality of the model in your initial sketch. Knowing there will be a rest break makes this sketch crucial in success of the paintng. The model for this watercolor is an older woman who understands the art of modeling and considers the needs of the entire class as she selects her poses.

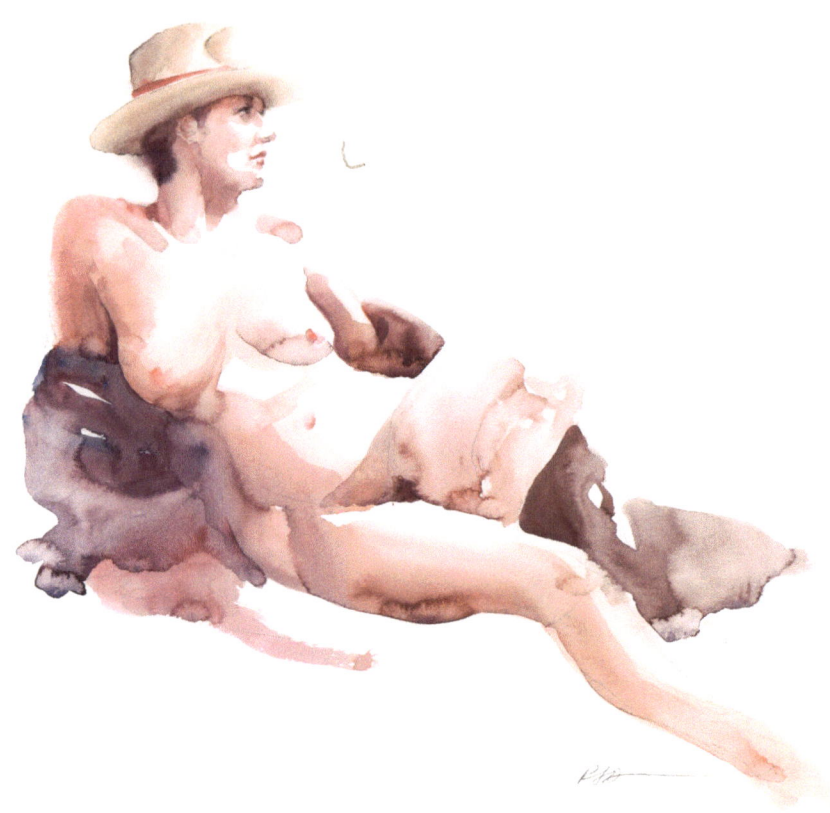

**Nude in a Fur Coat** was painted on a cold winter day when the model purposely brought a fur coat to class and used it to keep warm while posing. The result, above, is one of my favorite images. The painting below, done quickly, is typical of a difficult pose. Looking at the head upside down and trying to draw it correctly presents real challenges. We are so used to looking at the head, or even the body, head on, that upside down sketching is difficult.

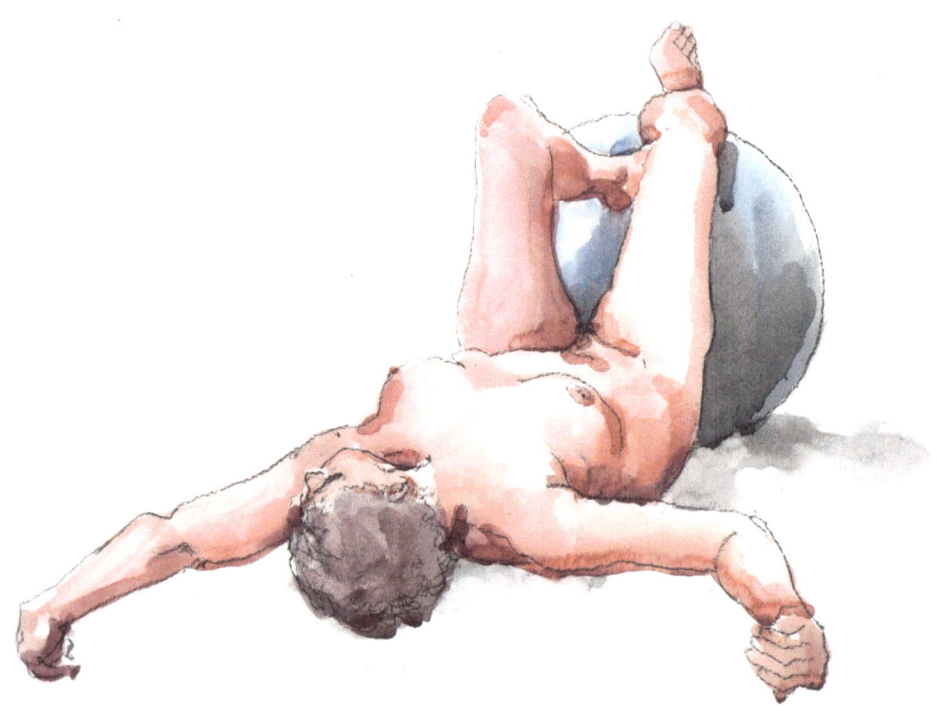

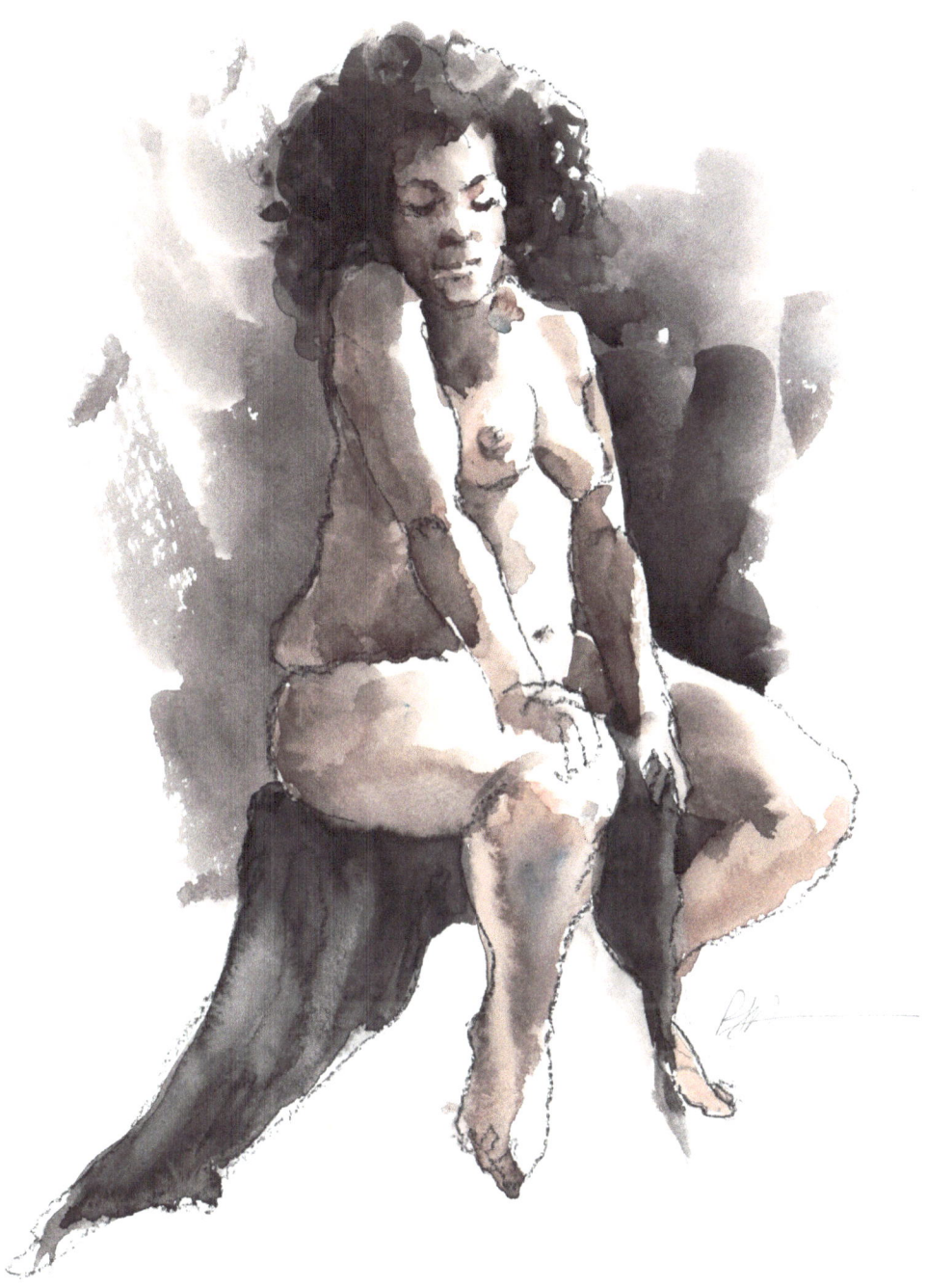

No need to go to full color on a long pose. Skin color is definitely hard to match with paint. Black and brown skin, in particular, is difficult to capture. People of color have the luxury of many shades, hues, and tones. Cosmetic companies have struggled with this for years and while it is a challenge you will face in life class, it is one to be embraced. Start out simply with a limited palette knowing that we are all different and no formula or recipe for mixing colors or describing skin tones will ever suffice for everyone.

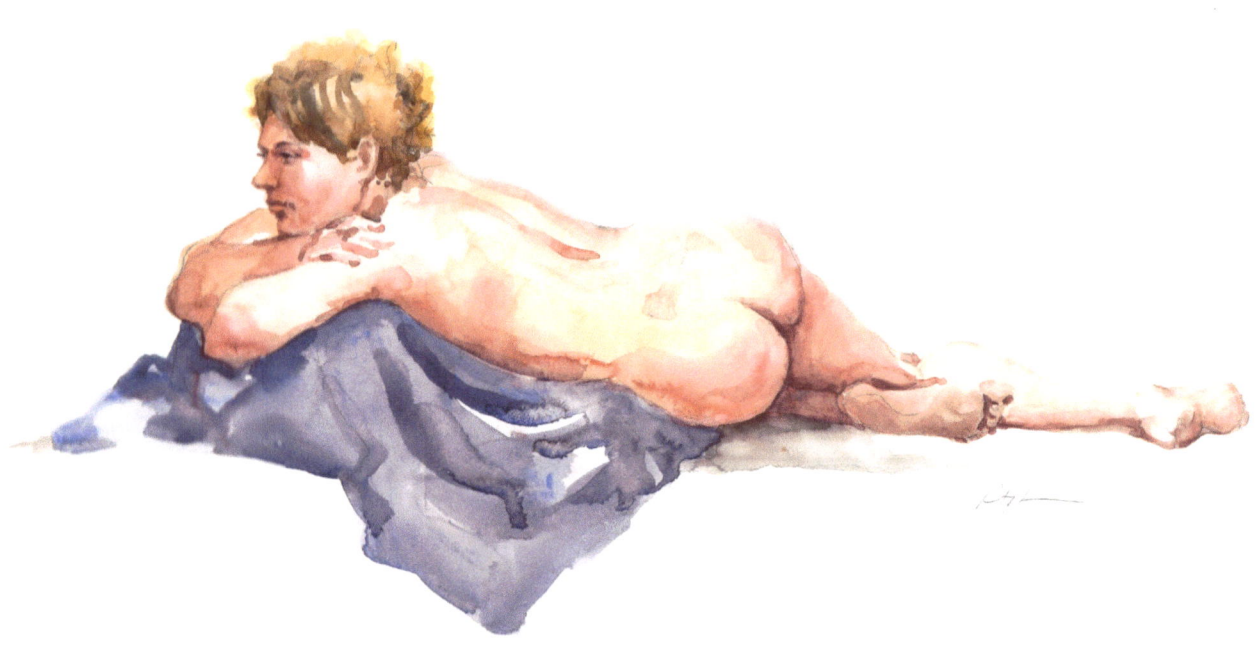

When you have had success drawing and painting a model it is always a joy when the same model shows up again for life class. The poses just seem "right" and you leave the session feeling pleased with what you have accomplished. Some models just have a better understanding of the needs of an artist than others. This model was always fun to draw.

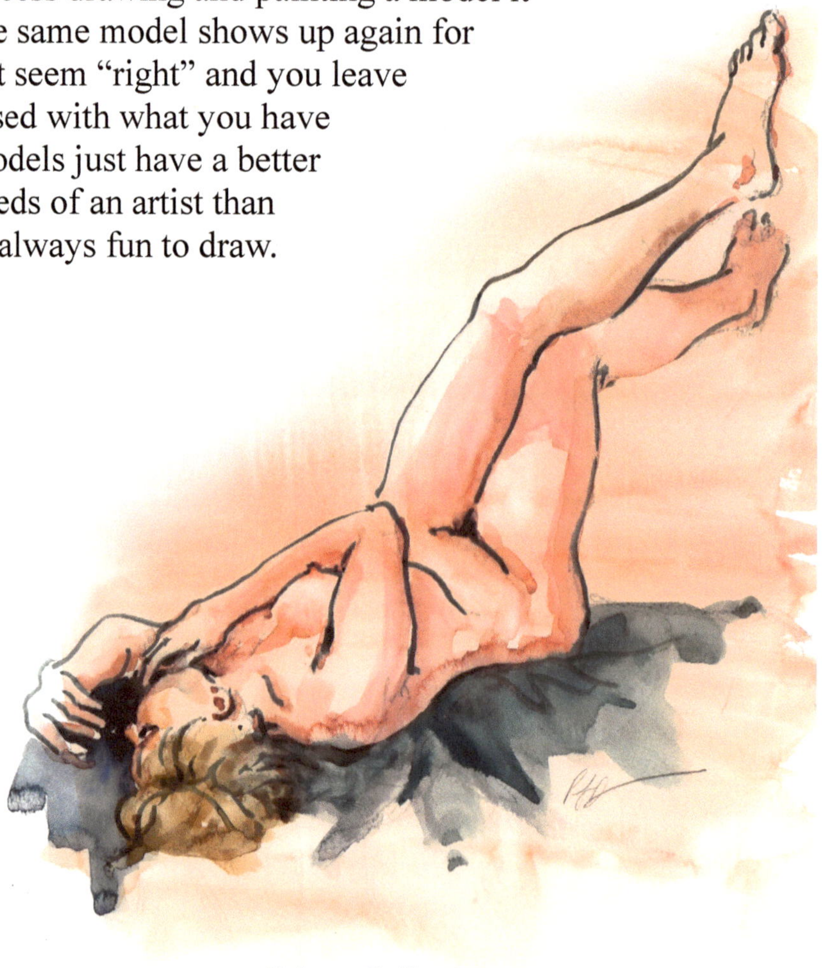

Private Collection

An hour is certainly not time enough for a careful, finished painting, but this is not the time for anything but trying to build upon and learn from your class experience – from the short poses to a long pose or two at the end of the session.

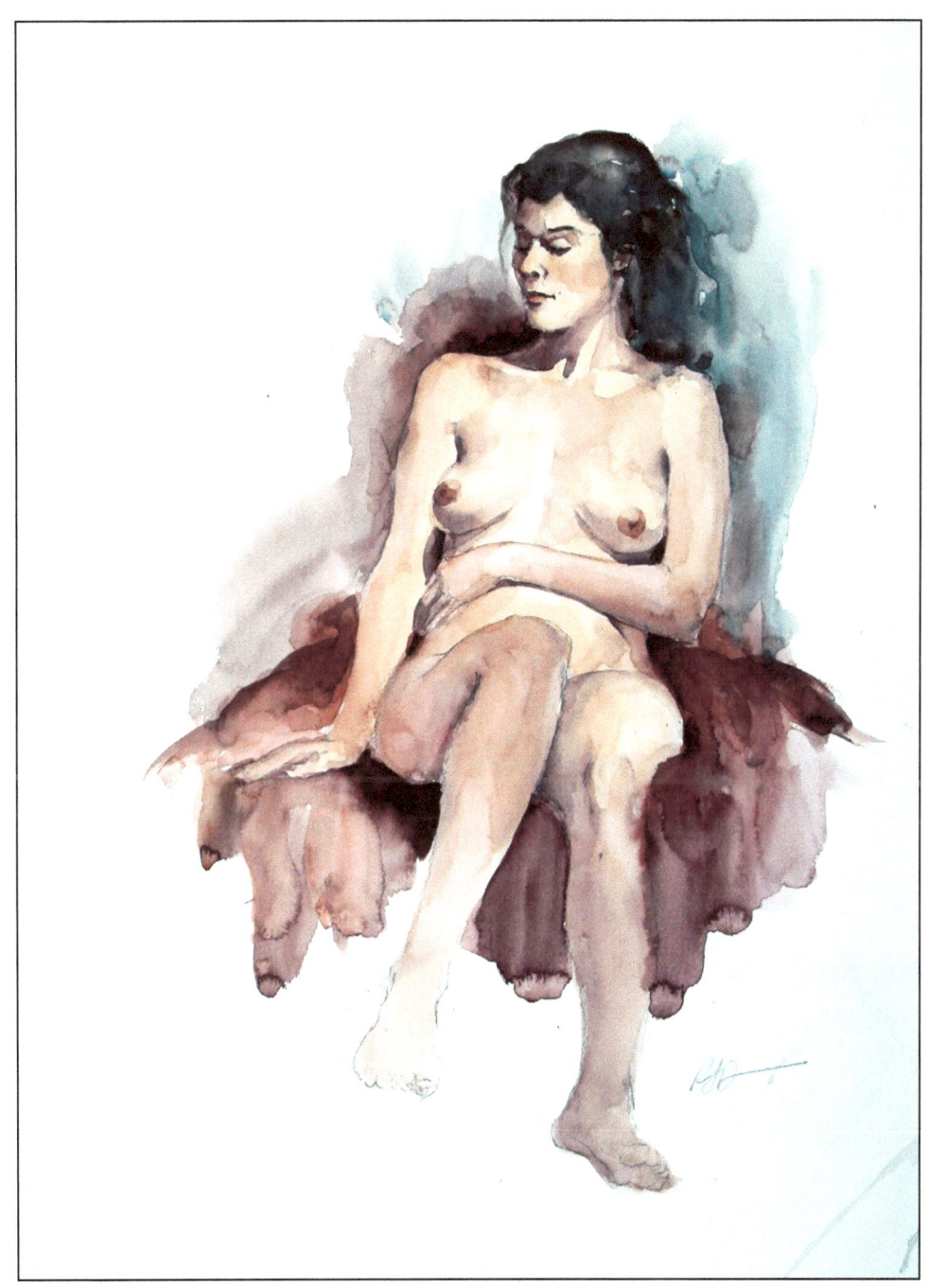

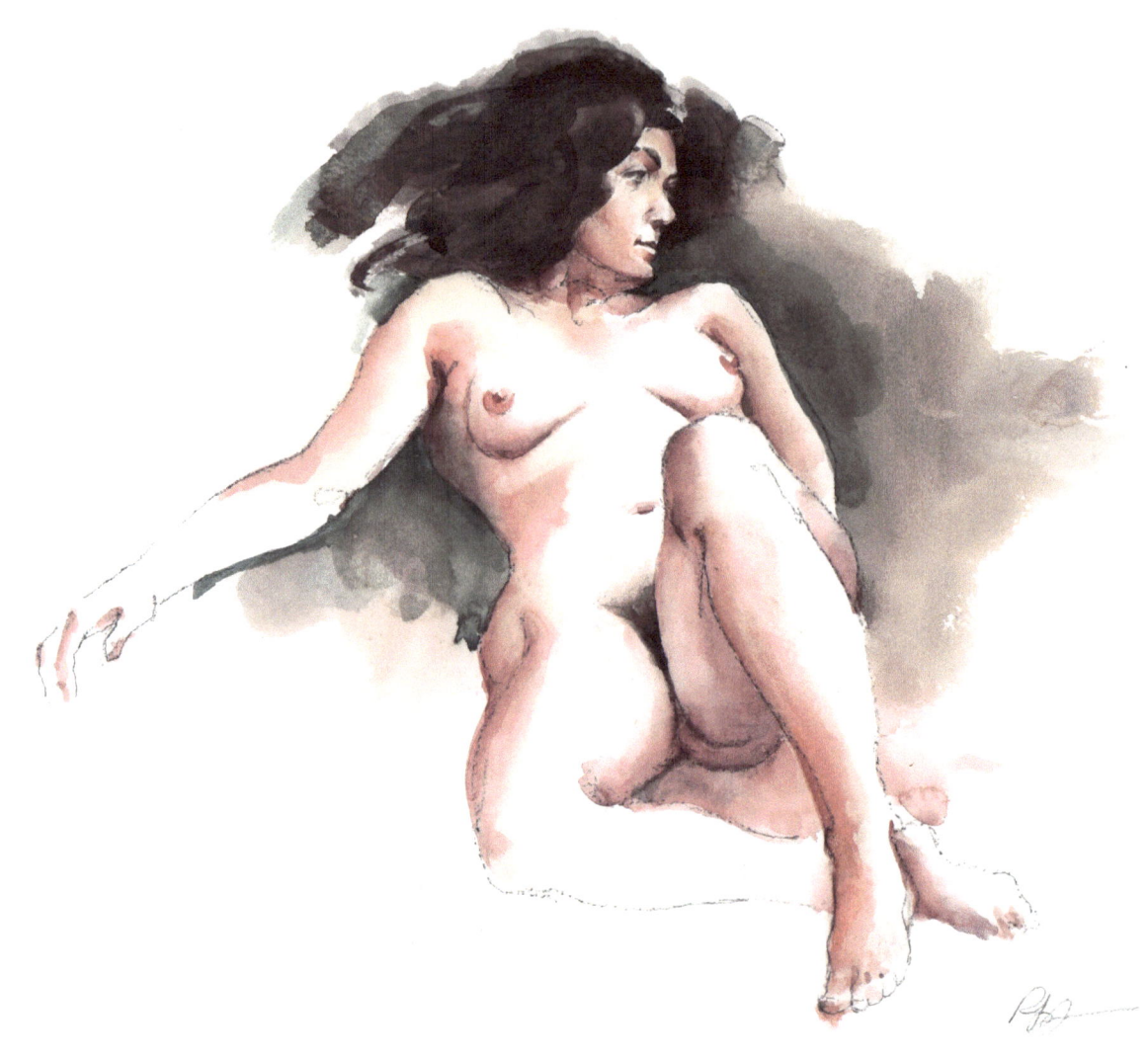

This hour long pose was done with a little too much concern for exactitude and not enough brush stroke abandon. Each week we bring a different mood to class. Sometimes, when things are going well, we can paint freely, and at other times we feel uptight. Navigating moods and health and finances... the list is long and every day is a little different from the day before. You can't hide behind your painting.

# The Gallery

The purpose of this book is to help you draw and paint convincing figures. I have found that interest in a painting is enhanced by the inclusion of a figure or figures. It should come as no surprise that people like to look at paintings that include people. I try, whenever possible, to include people that will enhance my paintings. And, if you are a plein air painter it will introduce you to an exciting new world.

# The Gallery

The goal of this book is to help you produce convincing figures for inclusion in your paintings. Irrespective of medium, a convincing figure can make a great deal of difference in the effectiveness of your artwork. Too many paintings fail because the figure or figures look awkward, and, simply, unreal. Instead of improving a landscape, poorly realized figures can undermine its effectiveness. Too often a figure looks like it was included as an afterthought.

## Trout Stream Idyll (acrylic)

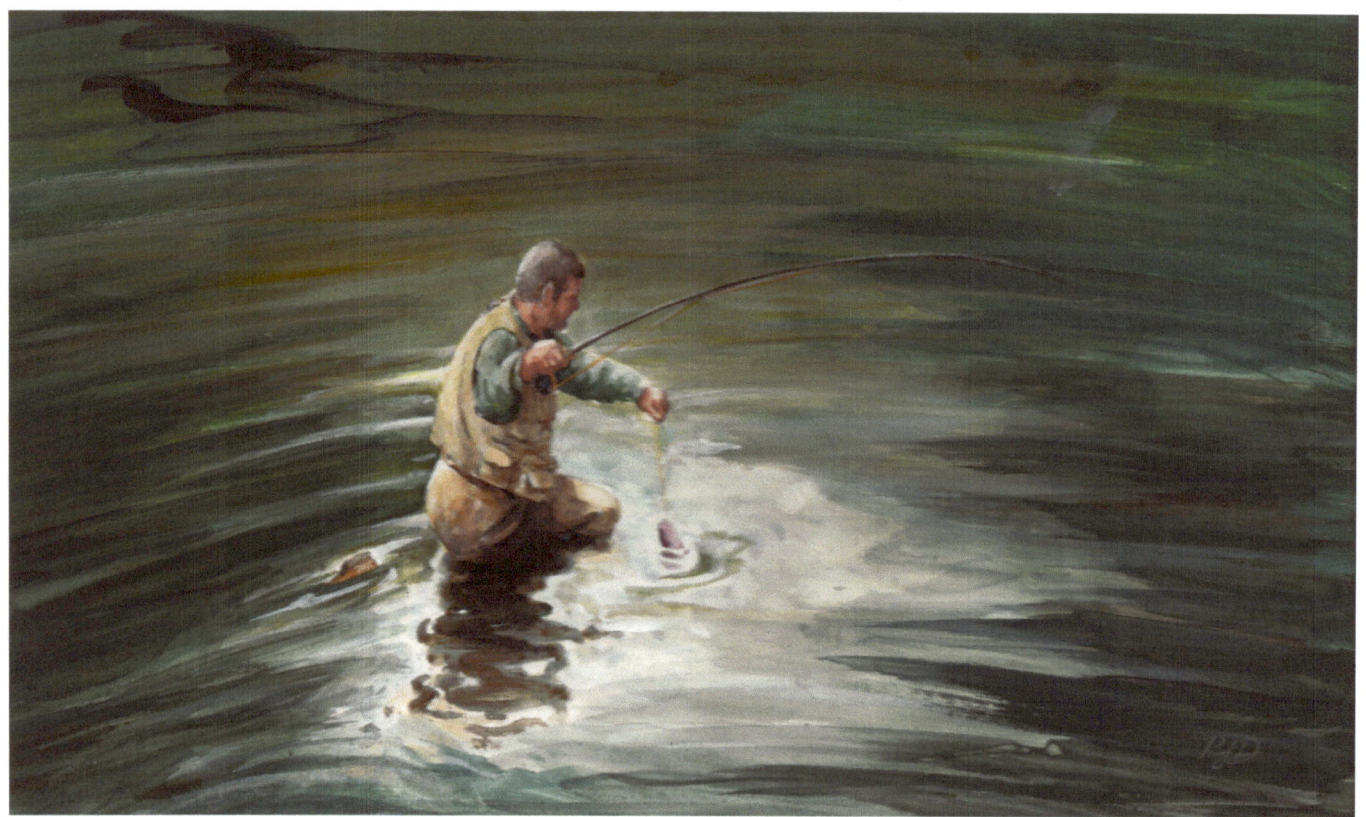

For me, this painting serves as a remembrance of a perfect day, fishing a tree-covered New Jersey stream in mid-summer. My fishing partner, painted kneeling in a shallow area, is about to "land" a trout and carefully release it. By kneeling he can exert more control during the release, so as not to injure the fish. I think his immersive pose emphasized his love of the sport of fishing.

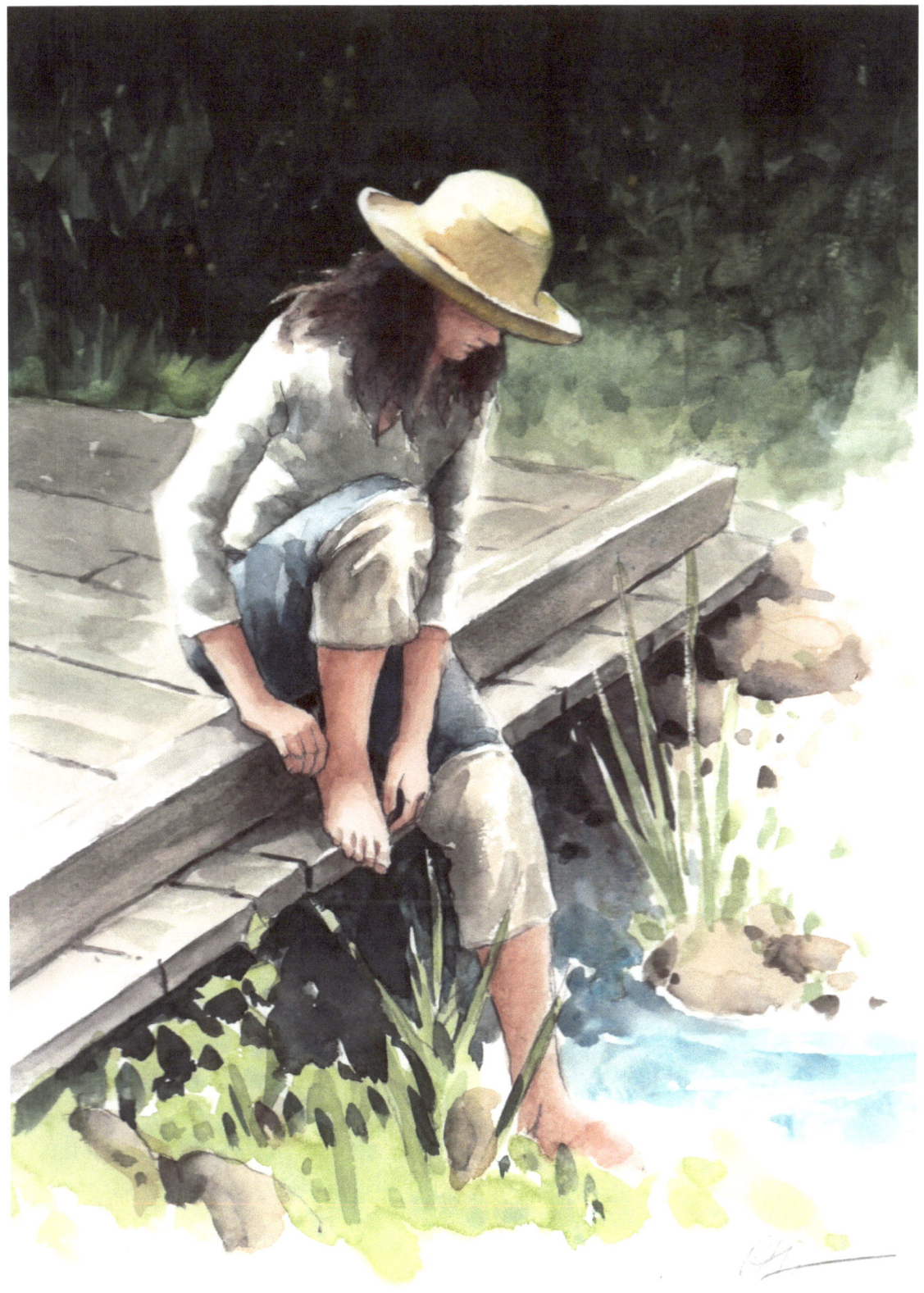

**Summer Idyll.** A small stream in western North Carolina was the perfect setting for a barefooted, lovely young lady on a perfect summer afternoon.

Private collection

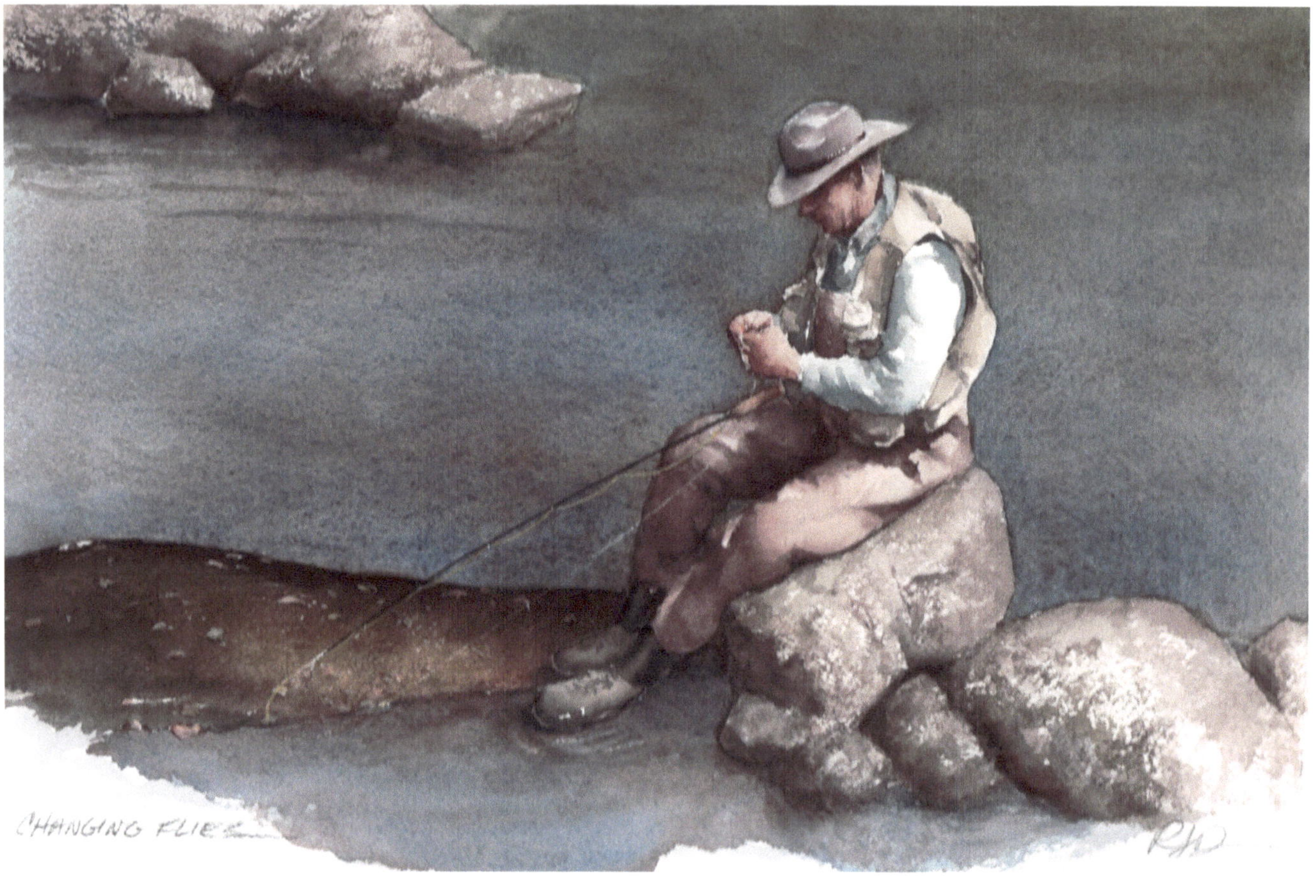

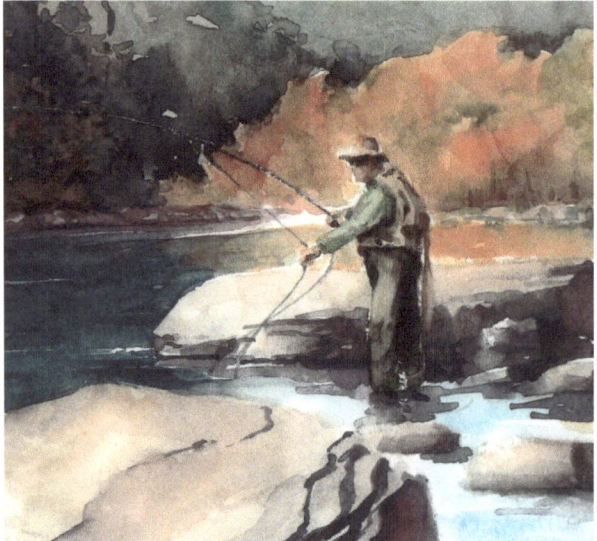

CHANGING FLIES

**Changing Flies.** This is a watercolor of a good friend and fellow fly fisherman changing flies on a little brook in New Jersey. When painting a fly fishing picture, I always use someone who knows the sport. Too many pictures of otherwise pleasant river scenes are ruined by the inclusion of a poorly realized figure, particularly an awkward figure of a novice fisherman. Sportsmen are the main audience (and clients) for sporting paintings and they can spot the uninformed artist who dares paint a sporting scene about which he knows little. Once you find a good, experienced model, know you have a precious resource.

The inset is from a painting on the famous Beaverkill River in New York, under different conditions than we found at the above stream. It is the fall of the year and it was a great day for fishing or painting – or both.

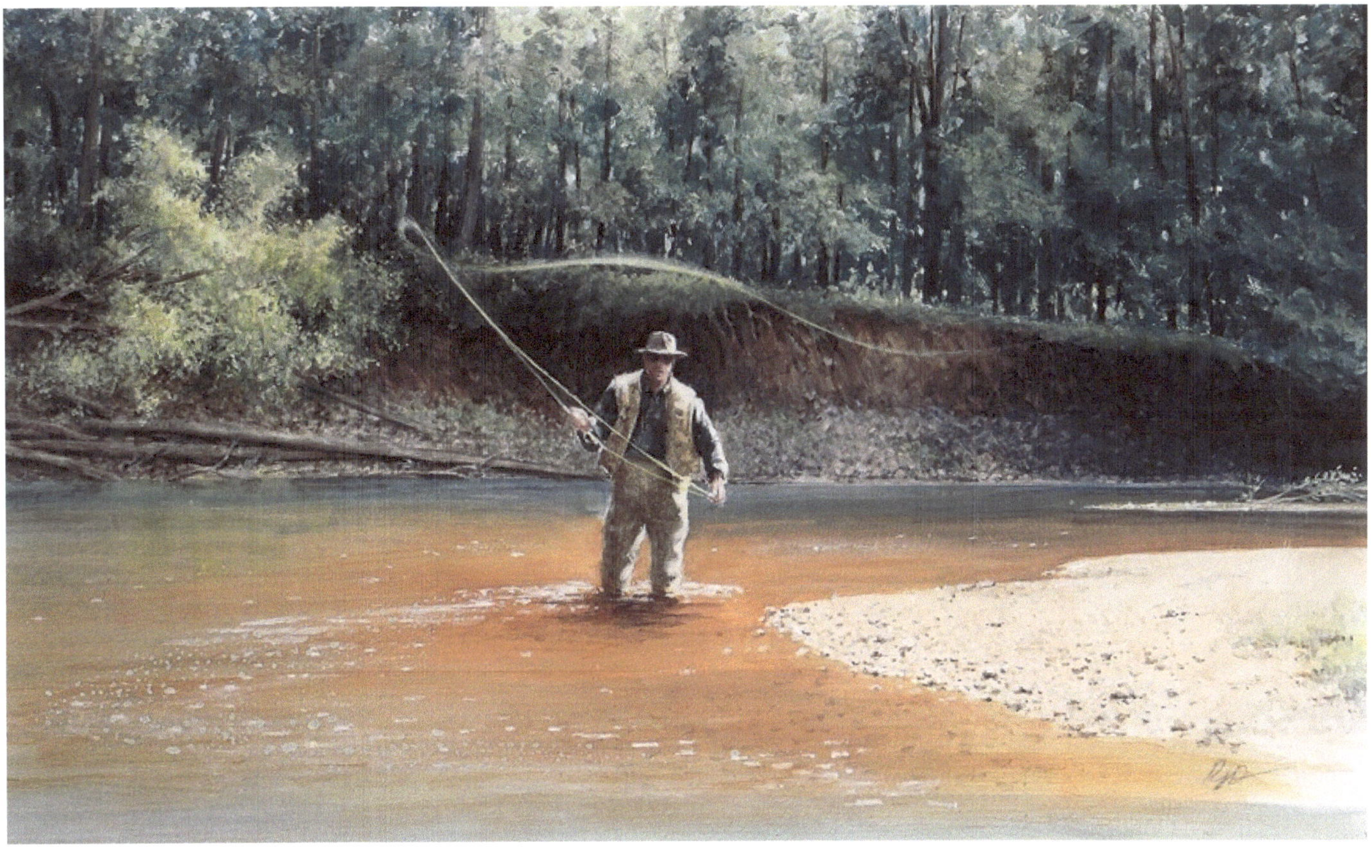

Private collection

One of my favorite fishermen posed for **Fishing on the Roundout Creek** in New York, near Kingston. The undercut riverbank serves as a perfect backdrop for the sunlighted figure. Artistically, the dark bank works to highlight the figure, caught in the act of casting a fly in this well known trout stream. A prospective client, usually a fisherman himself, can tell immediately, whether or not the fisherman shown is handling the line properly, as he makes a cast.

This painting was used for a poster promoting my solo show at the Belskie Museum of Art & Science in New Jersey.

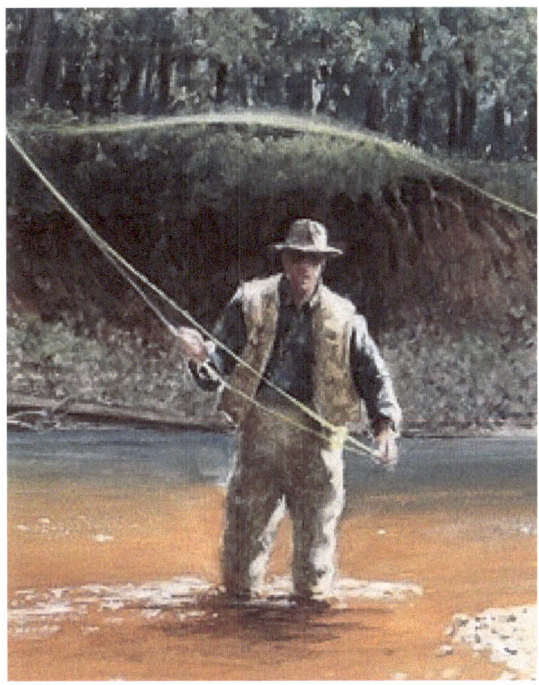

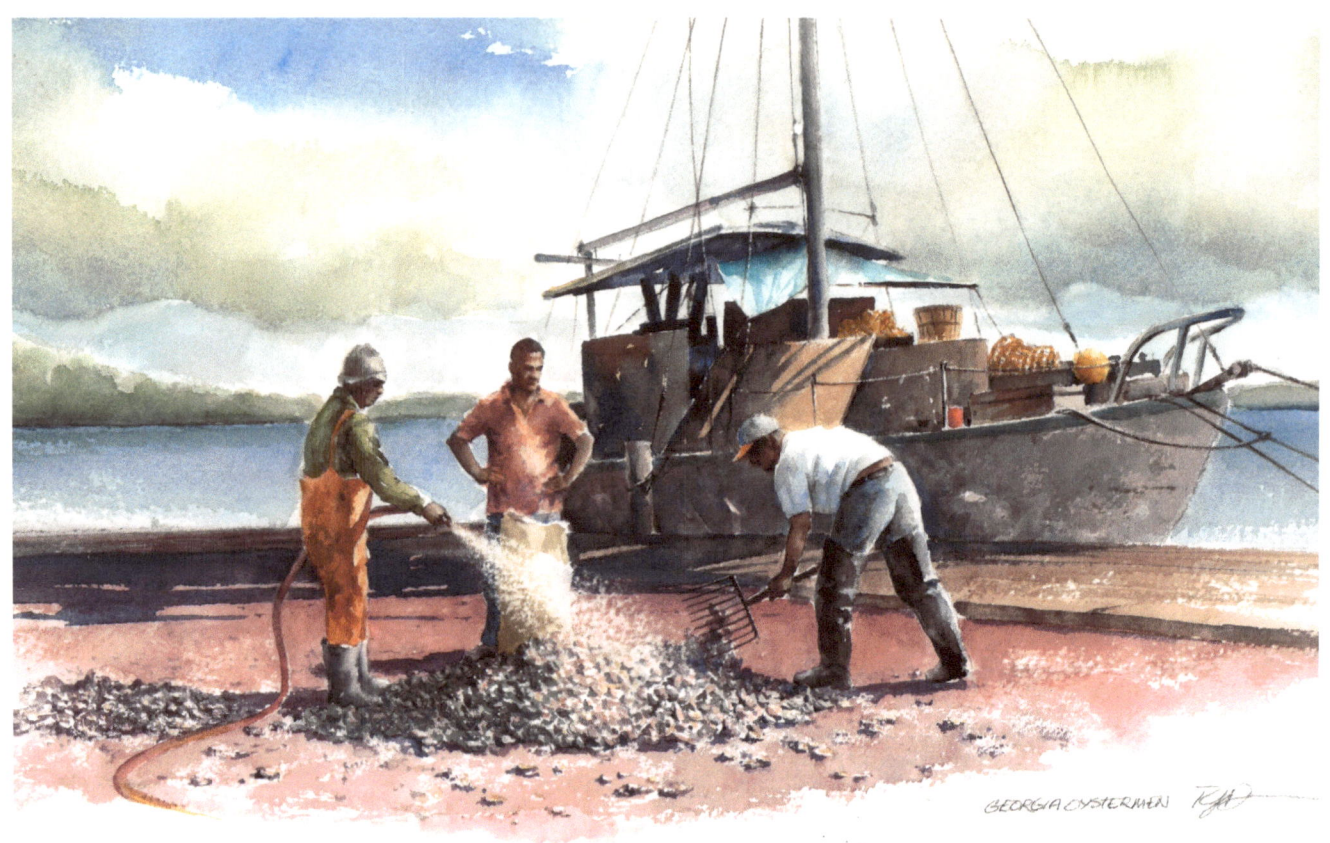

GEORGIA OYSTERMEN

**Georgia Oyster Pickers.** The painting shows itinerant oystermen cleaning and sorting their haul before bagging and selling them to an oyster distributor in Bluffton S.C. This scene is on the famous May River and the oysters from the May are delicious and prized by oyster lovers everywhere. These men ply the river on their boat, and in additon to harvesting oysters, they may collect items

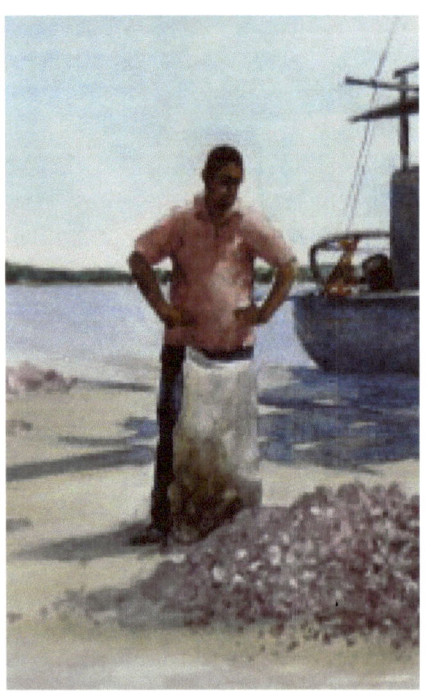

of value that happen to float by (note the large sheet of plywood on the deck). Their boat made a colorful backdrop for my painting. Without the figures I would have had just another boat painting, of which I have many. This is one more example of the value of including active people in your work.

I couldn't resist repainting the scene just to capture the sunlight on that bag of oysters.

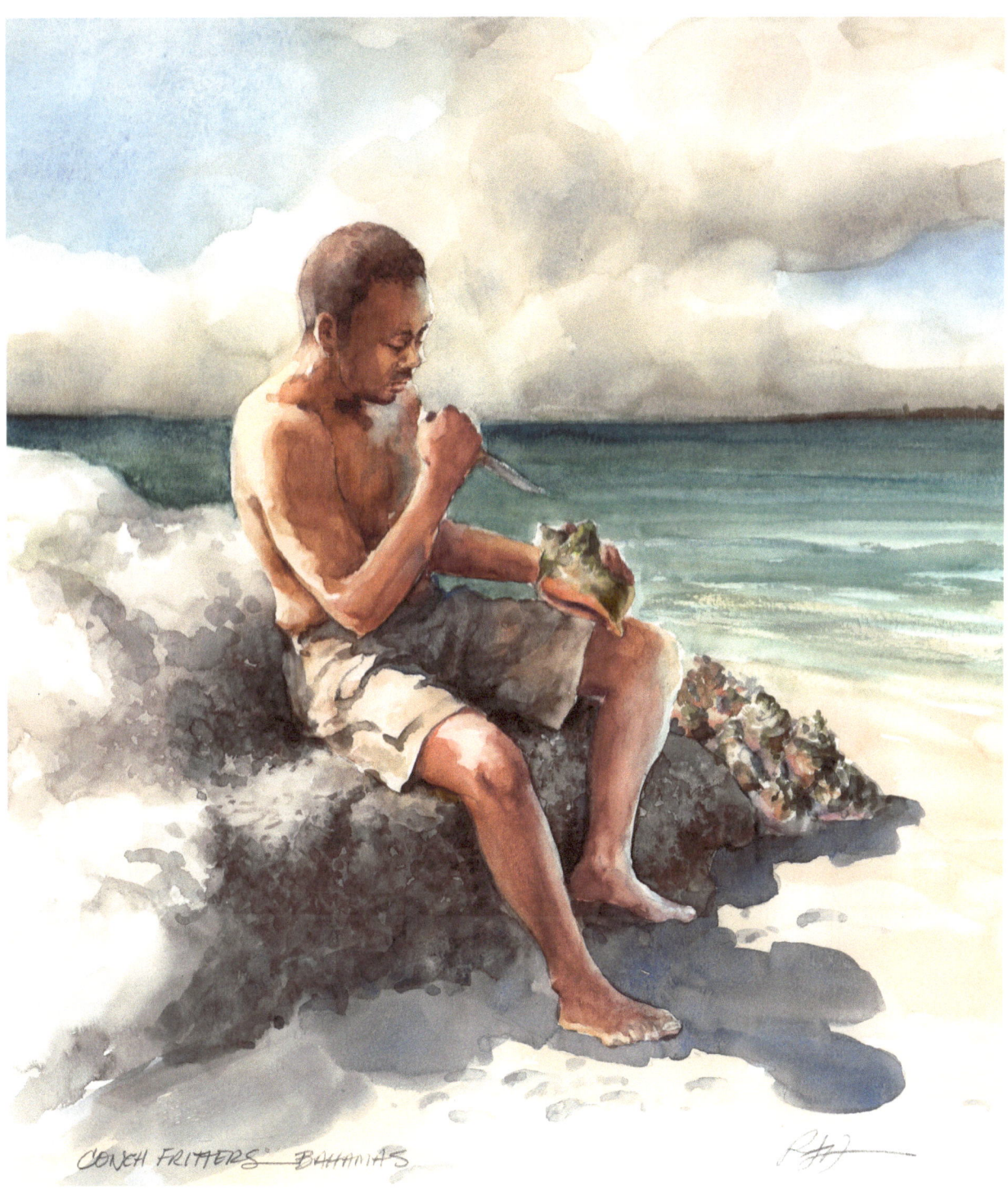

CONCH FRITTERS: BAHAMAS

**Conch Fritters** was painted, in plein air, on a Caribbean island. The man, a native islander, was harvesting Queen Conch for conch fritters and marinated conch. I told him that I was an artist, and asked if he would pose for me. I offered him a small fee. What did I want him to do? I said, just continue doing what you are doing. I have found that artists, being non-threatening, are often greeted with friendliness, rather than suspicion. The proper approach can lead to a great pose.

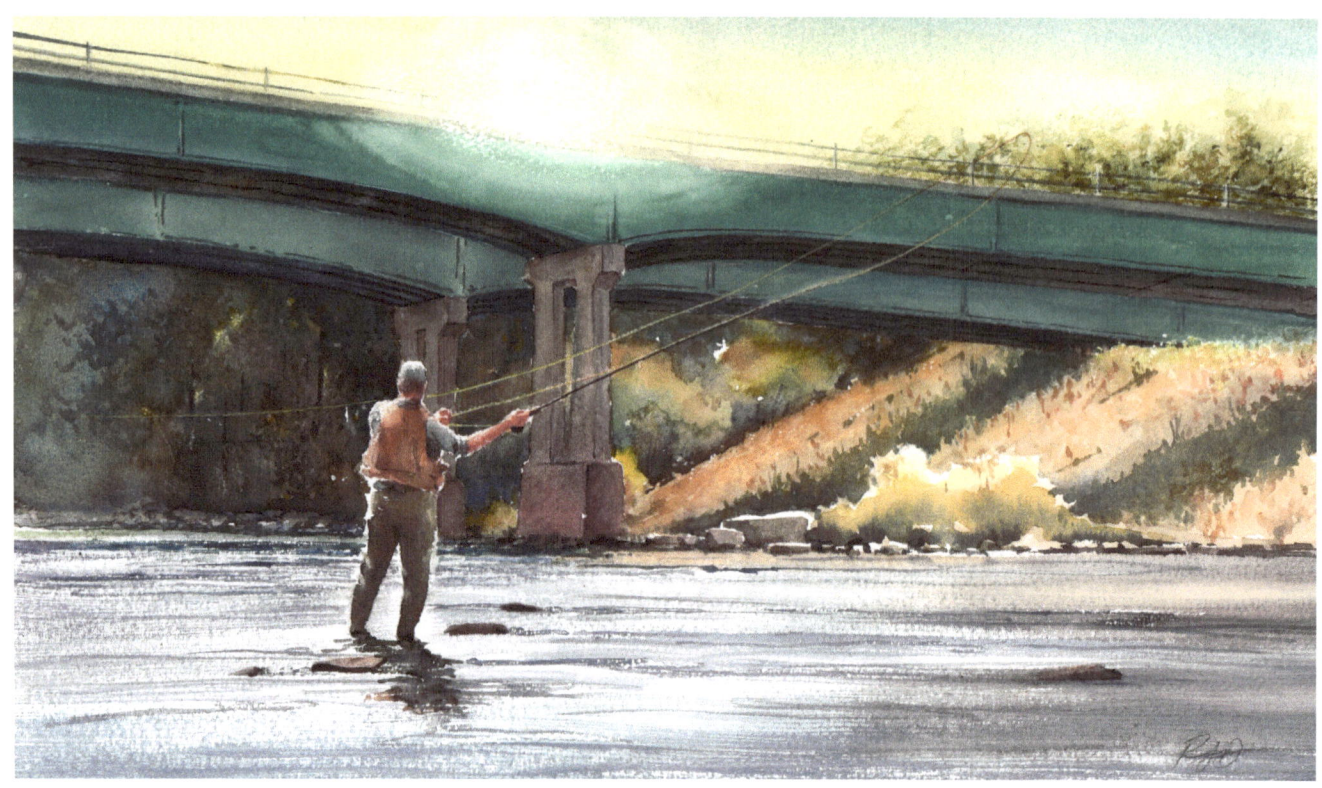

**Cairn's Pool** is a storied trout pool on the Beaverkill River, near Roscoe, N.Y. Driving along the Route 17 Quickway always demands a quick look at the river as you cross it, above Cairn's Pool. Winter, summer, spring, or fall, you will usually see a stalwart fisherman or two trying his luck there. Springs near the far shore provide a steady supply of the cool water that the trout need and love, and the fishermen know that the trout are there, near the springs. In this painting, the sun is above and behind the fisherman, creating a nice halo effect around the figure. No worry about the figure getting lost, or the composition suffering, with nature working for you. Painting water is always a challenge. It is never the same. Weather, time of day, time of year, clouds, or sun, all make for infinite variety. Blue, of course, reads as water, but painting it blue all the time is an untruth.

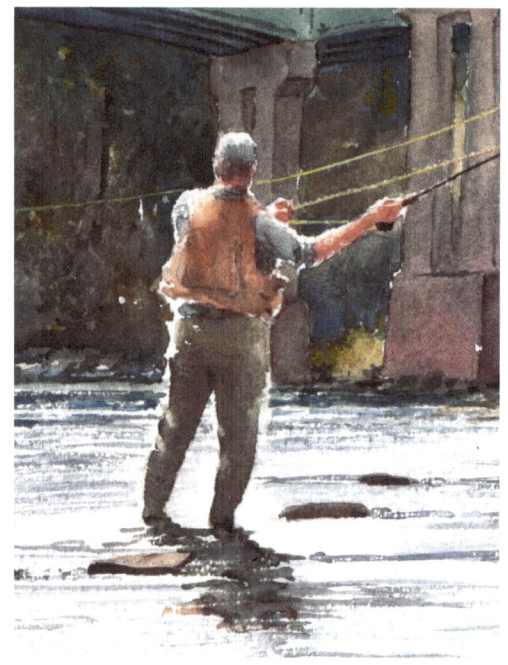

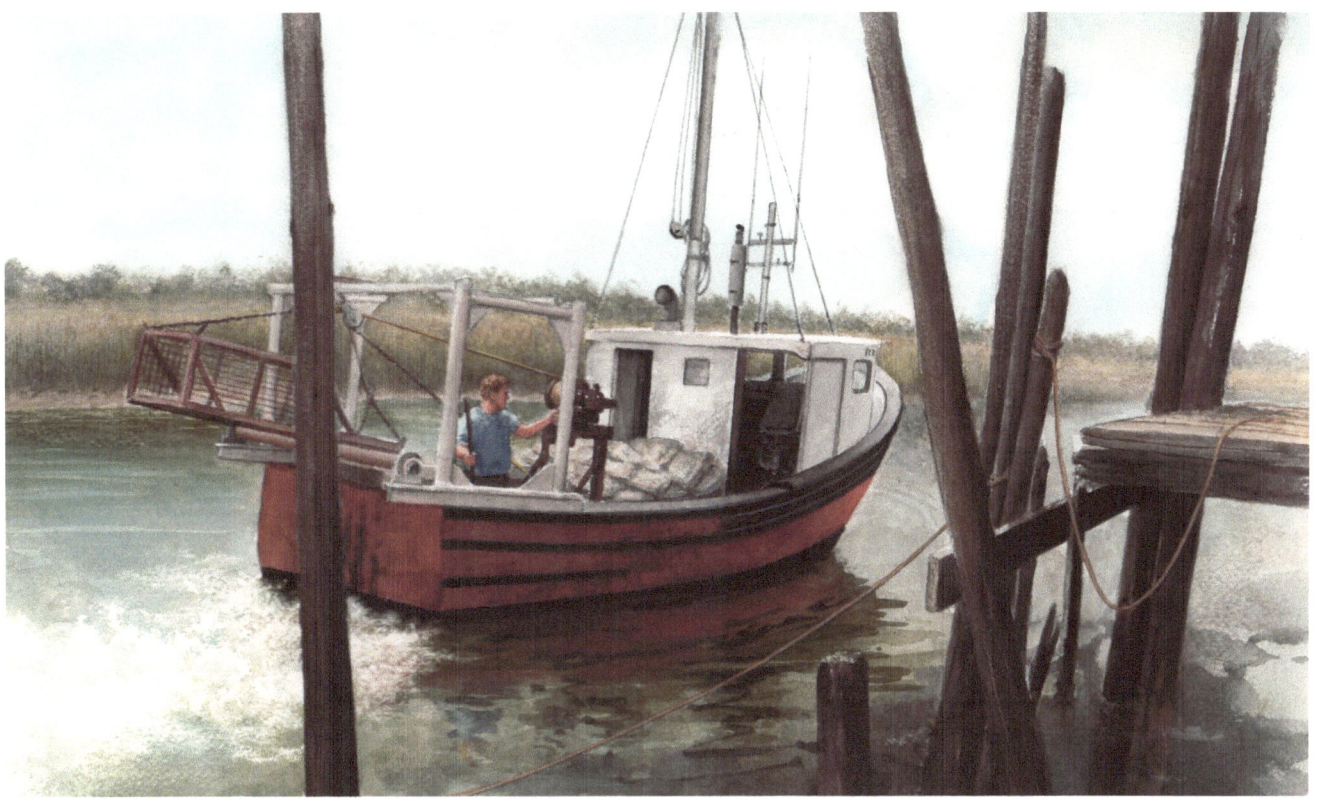

**Clam Harvest.** Compton Creek, NJ is the location of a commercial fishing community that has existed since the Revolutionary War. It prospered as the population of New York City grew and became a major supplier of fish for the Fulton Fish Market for over a hundred years. Over-fishing and pollution have had a deleterious effect on the community and its future. However, it is still a mecca for artists. This painting shows a clam boat arriving with its harvest of clams, to be sold for the fishing bait market. Sadly, the clam beds are off–limits for human consumption, due to pollution from the rivers emptying into the Raritan Bay area.

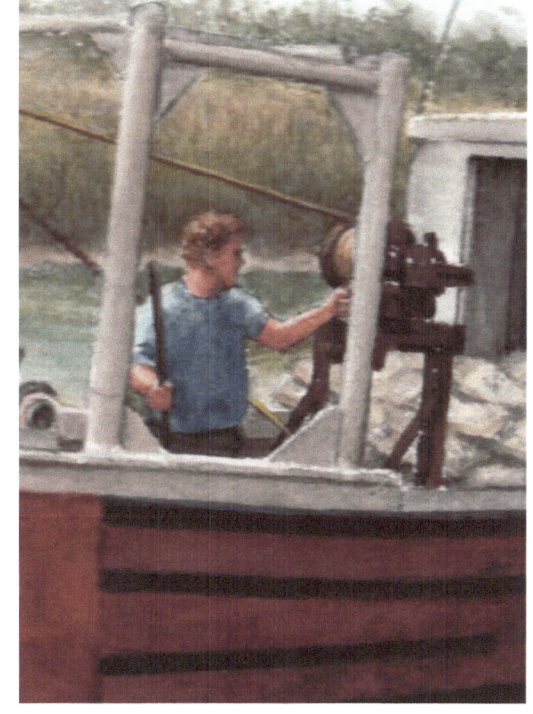

After painting a great many boats in this creek, I soon realized the need for interest beyond what the boats alone could supply. I needed people. Real people doing interesting jobs make a big difference. I found the community friendly, and as long as I didn't get in their way, they welcomed my interest in them and their work, and appreciated my paintings.

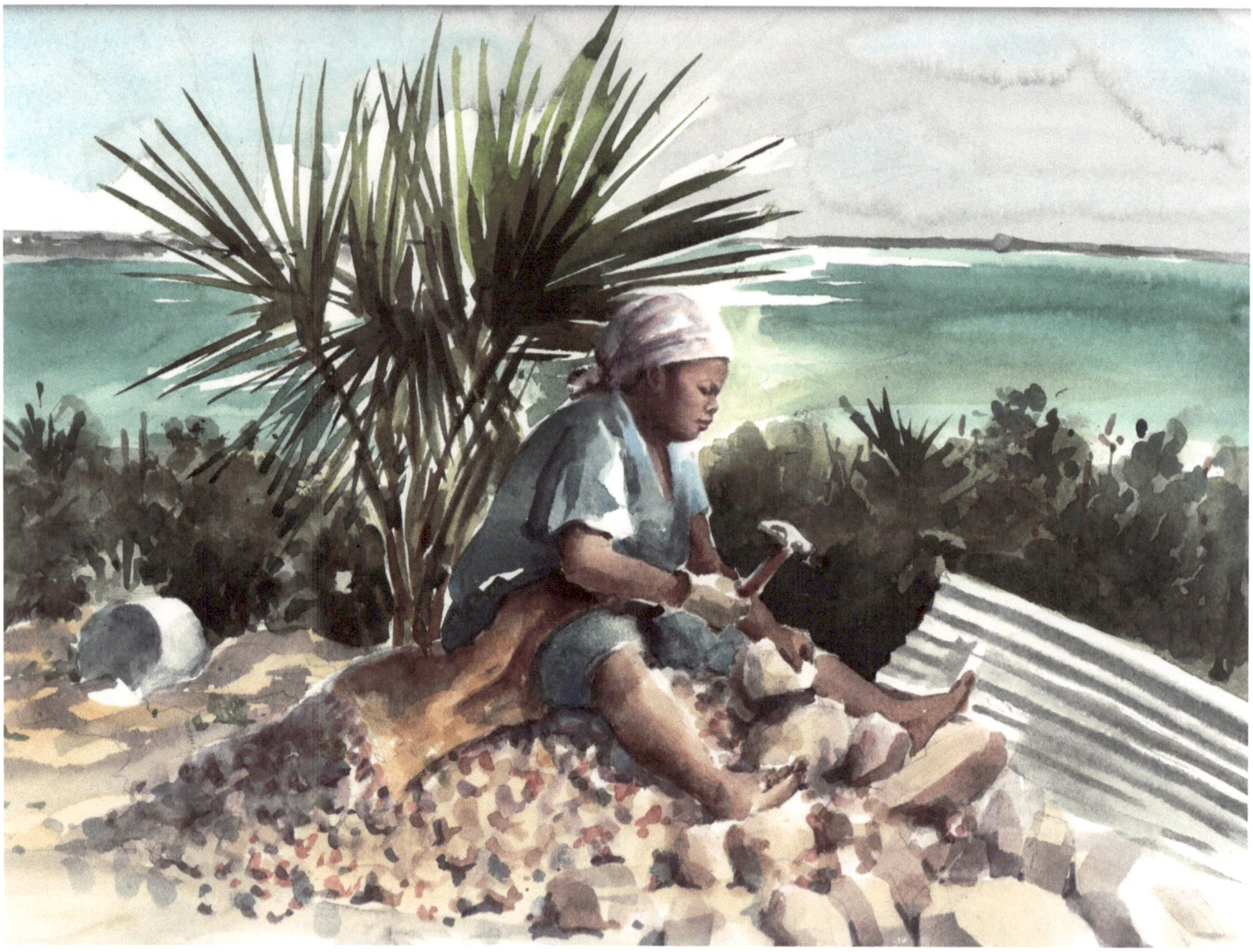

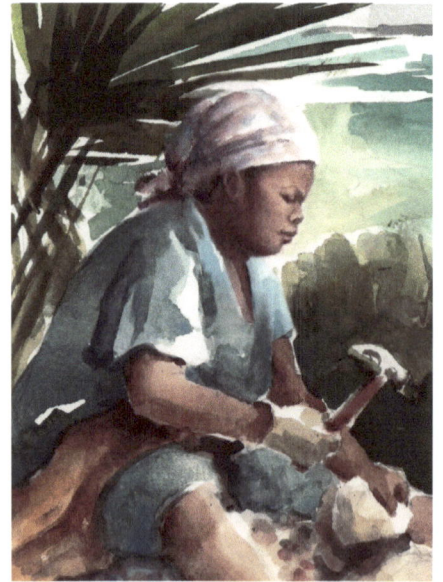

**Caribbean Mom.** A good part of my love of plein air painting is dealing with the people that one meet. This woman, a Caribbean native, supplemented her income by breaking up coral rock for use by the local builders. Her boys would bring her large pieces of coral and she would hammer them into usable size for cement construction on the island. She didn't earn a great deal of money, so she was anxious, but wary of my offer of a few dollars, if she would pose. The usual exchange ensued: "What do you want me to do?" "Just keep doing what you are doing." She allowed me little more than an hour, so I had to paint fast. We quickly became friends, and as I drove by during the rest of the week she would wave and point me out to her neighbors and companions.

It's times like this that your experience with quick figure work pays off. Even if it is not a "painting trip" don't travel without a sketch pad. There are too many memorable occasions just waiting to be discovered.

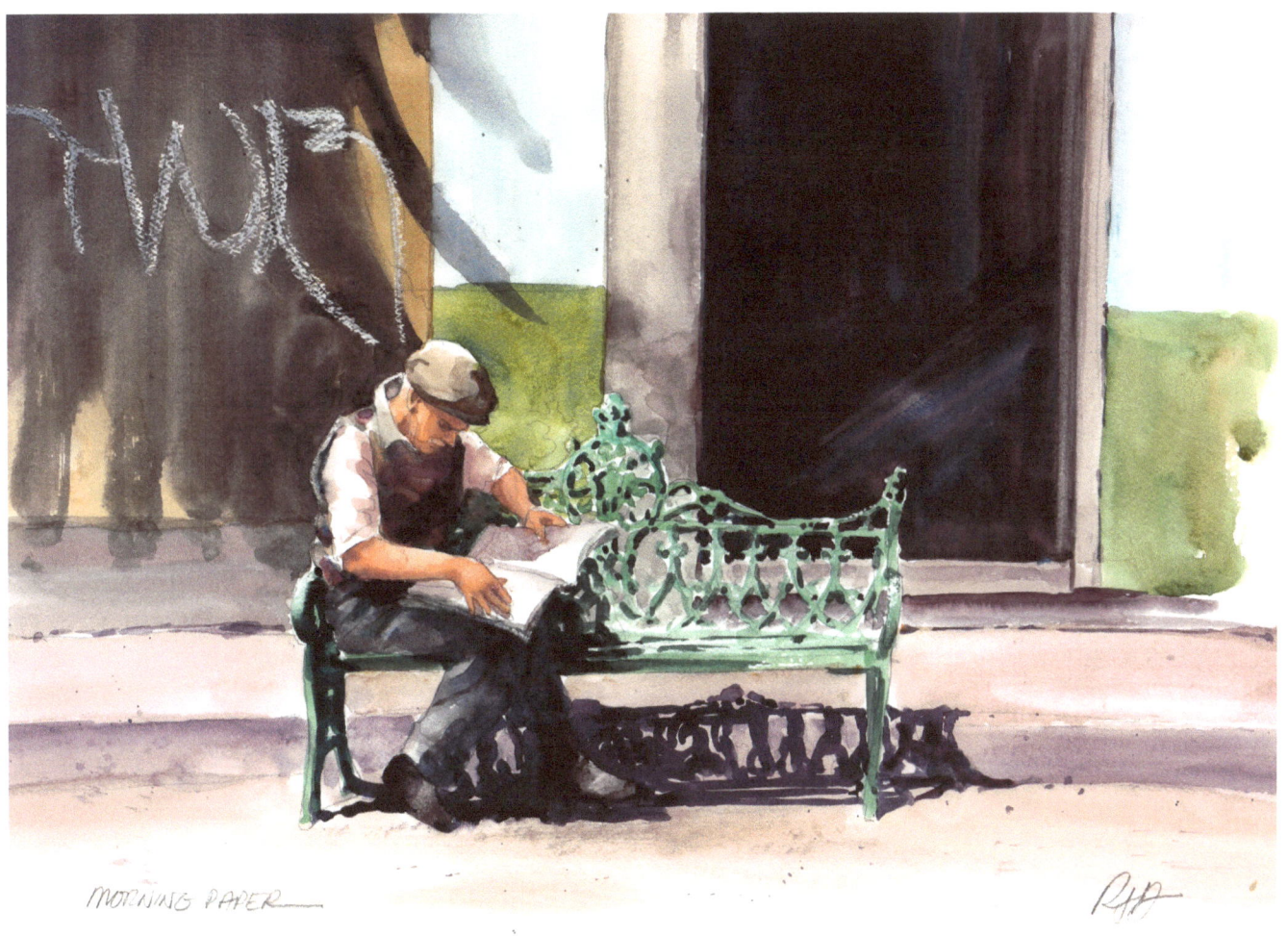

MORNING PAPER

**Morning Paper.** Reading the morning paper is a universal occurence, but that doesn't mean that it is not a good subject for a painting. I came across this gentleman in Guadalajara, Mexico. He was totally absorbed in his newspaper, and yet he agreed to just keep reading, even while I was sketching him. I supplemented my sketches with some photographs and bid him "Good day" (in Spanish). I loved the cast-iron settee and had fun painting its intricate tracery on the back support, with a shield in the center. Upon returning home I was surprised to see the bench featured in an article in the New York Times. It was produced by the Coalbrookdale Company in England, about 1860. This unique pattern is, purportedly very rare. The article was accompanied by a photograph of "my" settee. What a treat! I only wish I had known of this while I was in Mexico. What fun it would have been to share this information, not only with my fellow travelers, but with this Guadalajaran gentleman. This just another example of the rewards of painting en plein air.

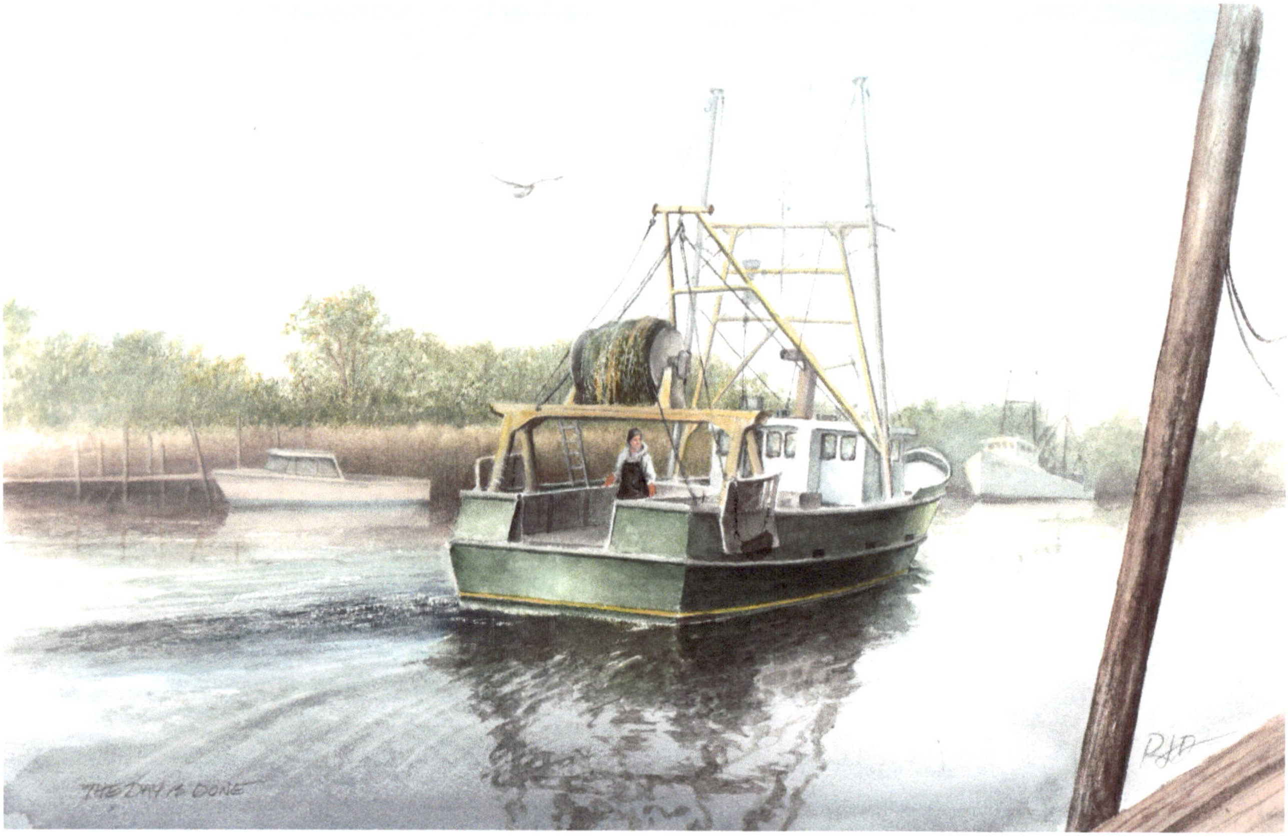

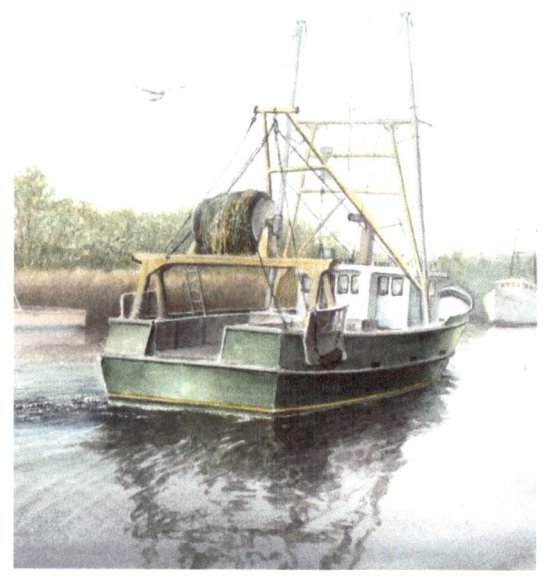

## The Importance of the Figure

Having painted a great many scenes without a figure, it took me too long to realize how much more interesting a painting is when one or more figures are included. It's an obvious observation. People like to observe other people. The above painting shows a commercial fishing boat heading for the dock after it unloaded it's day's catch. The inset show the same painting with the fisherman removed for comparison purposes.

# Post Script
## *Painting in Plein Air*

As you have read, I love to paint in plein air and while you can't paint outside all the time, I worry about the value of classes where the student is asked to bring a favorite photograph to be used as the subject to be painted. The photograph is a Still Life – and will be copied, as a vase on a table or a basket of fruit is copied. Encourage your instructor to take your class out of doors whenever practical.

A photograph is two dimensional. Most of the composition, such as it is, is before you. A scene from which you find it difficult to escape. Even if you do it well, you just have a copied photograph. The values are presented to you as the camera saw them. It is hard to look into a shadow in many photographs. On site,

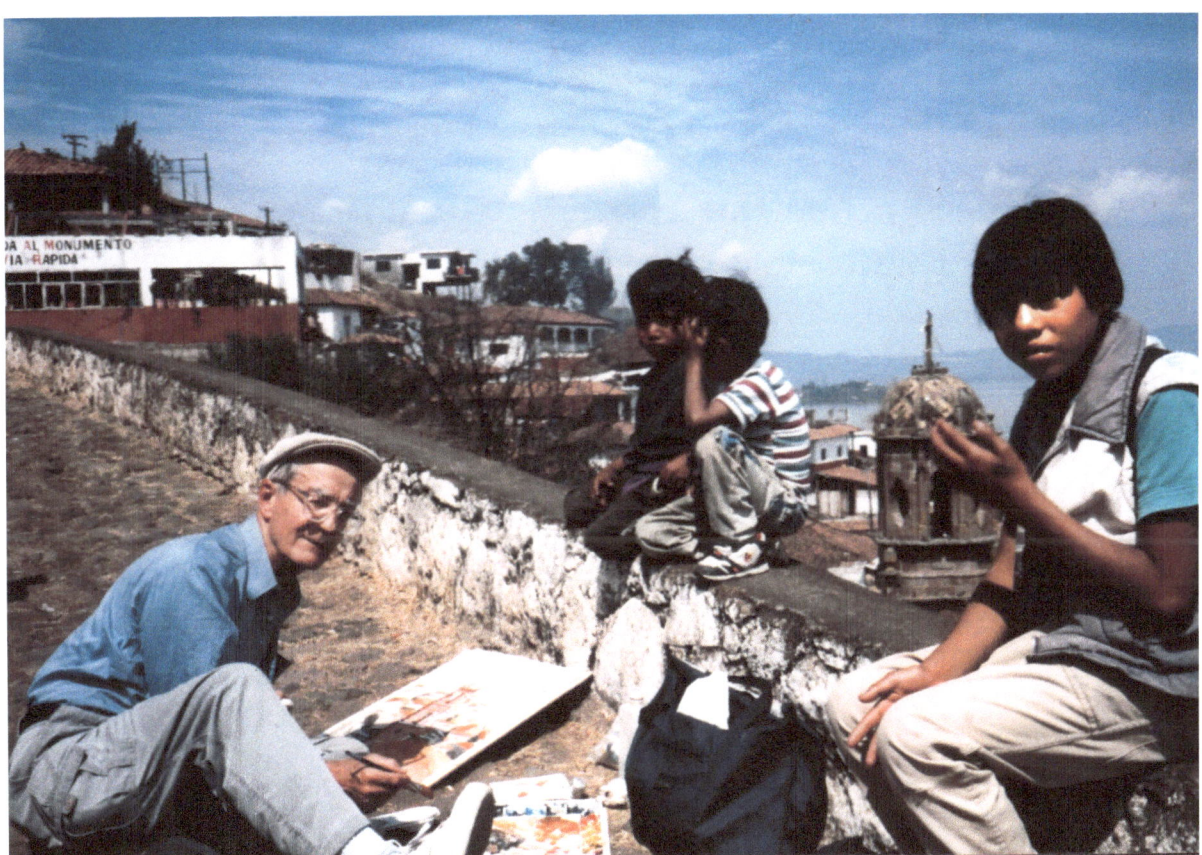
The author, painting in Mexico, with the local kids as an audience.

the eye can accomodate to the dark and see more. It is also impossible to look around an object the way you can on site. When you are there you can walk over to the left or right to get a better view of your subject. You can't include a bush or that boat that was just outside the scope of your photograph because you no longer have the scene in front of you. In short, you are imprisoned by that little black box called a camera.

Now, I am not being two-faced about this. I, too, use a camera. I shoot hundreds of photographs. My files are full of them. Most are useless. Some are essential. What makes the difference?

Often, you can't return to the same place again. The time of day, the weather conditions, the sunlight, clouds, and that intangible feel for the place, is always different. Your photos can act as support if you take plenty of pictures of things not in the scene, or things just outside the scene, and use different exposures. More details will often show up. Expose for the shadows. Andrew Wyeth's success, to a large extent, lies in his ability to let you look into his shadows. He uses shadows a great deal to enhance his composition. Notice how well his paintings "carry" across the room in a museum.

Often it is difficult to finish a watercolor at one sitting, so I note the exact time of day. If needed, I can return and capture some of the same conditions another day. Don't forget the enjoyment you will get from meeting the people when you paint outdoors. You will meet lots of people, and friendliness goes a long way.

**And did I mention that art is a universal language? It doesn't matter that you can't speak the local language. You are already communicating with them by being there ...and painting.**

In France, I had a lady drag a chair across the road for me to sit on because I was sitting on the curb and she thought I was uncomfortable. I heard the noise first, and as I watched her approach I couldn't imagine why she was dragging that chair. Well, the chair was for me and I thanked her profusely and dutifully sat on it and finished the watercolor. My old curb seat put me closer to my paints and the reach from the chair was difficult but I never let her know that I was uncomfortable. My delight in her effort and her pleasant smile made my discomfort more than worth it.

Wherever I am, I find that the children also love artists. At times, I've had dozens of them crowd around and they are so interested that I often have to ask them to stop blocking my view. Sometimes the older boys will act as surrogates and help get the little ones to move out of my sight line. But be careful: give one of them a quick sketch and they all want one.

# About The Author

Robert Demarest has been interested in producing books and doing book illustration throughout his career. A recent book, *Traveling with Winslow Homer – America's Premier Artist/Angler* was the result of his following in Homer's footsteps over much of the Western World. Little did he know, when he started his odyssey, that Homer traveled so extensively. Demarest's quest led him as far as the North Sea Coast of England, and also to Cuba, Bermuda, both coasts of Florida and of course, Maine and Massachusetts, New York, and New Jersey.

Demarest's magnum opus was *Conception, Birth, and Contraception*, a book he conceived and then produced with Jack Sciarra. It was translated into five foreign language editions and later revised and republished by Parthenon Publishing as *Human Reproduction & Fertility Control* with Rita Charon as his co-author.

He recently produced a small booklet, *Abram Belskie, Sculptor - and the Famous America Sculptors with Whom He Worked*. He transfered the copywrite to the Belskie Museum in New Jersey so it could be sold for their benefit.

His medical illustrations now reside in the permanent archives at Columbia's Medical School. He also has been awarded the Crosby Medal by Johns Hopkins Medical School for his service to medicine.

## Books by Robert J. Demarest

*Conception, Birth & Contraception* with John Sciarra, M.D. McGraw-Hill Book Co. Two editions and 5 foreign language editions.
Republished by Parthenon Press as *Human Reproduction and Fertility Control* with Rita Charon, M.D.

*Traveling with Winslow Homer America's Premier Artist/Angler*. Apple Trees, L.L.C.

*Noback's Neuroanatomy* 7 editions, Strominger, Demarest & Lemle. Humana Press/ Springer.

*Abram Belskie, Sculptor*. Belskie Museum, publisher.